Rüdiger Schlömer

TYPOGRAPHIC KNITTING

FROM PIXEL TO PATTERN

Princeton Architectural Press · New York

Contents

Of Pixels and Stitches

We can hardly imagine using or designing type without the latest programs and tools. Typography and type design have come to form the basis of a new, digital craftsmanship. But those who would like to connect with the tactile side of their typographic practice can do so through knitting, a kind of analog program, if you will, that translates pixels into stitches.

Knitting type presents digital typography with a form of materialization that, unlike *rapid prototyping*, retains a certain measure of personal distinctness. It allows practical digital typography to be enhanced by texture, feel, warmth, wearability—and, last but not least, camaraderie, through knitting circles, for example.

People who knit letters or words experience a slowing down of the design process, a sensation familiar to stonemasons and intarsia artists (intarsia in knitting derives its name from the wood inlay technique—it is the process of fitting color fields together in a woven design). *Typeknitting* is typographic meditation, a kind of digital detox—albeit one that doesn't spurn digital technology but instead lends itself to it as a practical plane for reflection. And, incidentally, in doing so it also underlines the Latin origins of the word "digital"—from *digitus*, meaning "finger."

TEXTILE WRITING

Combining knitting and typography is first and foremost a mental exercise. *Typeknitting* demands constant translation between the physical knitting process and the optical result. The run of the yarn and design of the letter must be conceived differently than what the look of the resulting textile would suggest. In *typeknitting*, letters are knitted backward: from right to left and from bottom to top. Stitches don't have a basic square shape, nor do they fit exactly into the design grid of a pixel font. Stranded yarn that is not loose enough can sabotage a piece of work by pulling the knitted result too tight.

These idiosyncrasies in translation from design to product can be a hindrance when you expect letters to be simply knitted up as a one-to-one copy. As you explore the freedom inherent in *typeknitting* while also applying the rules of the knitting that you're used to, you will likely discover many exciting visual opportunities that would hardly spring to mind when designing on the computer.

Typeknitting combines the peculiarities of programming and calligraphy: on the one hand, it's technical, logical, and precise—and on the other, tactile, flowing, and organic. Like a polished stroke of the brush, an even row of stitches is the result of lots of practice by which the corresponding hand movements become second nature. It's no coincidence that knitting patterns look rather mechanical, like pixel diagrams. A knitting pattern is a universal visual code that lends form to the variables of knit and purl stitches. The symbols of this cryptography can be universally decoded no matter what language you speak.

DIGITAL-ANALOG WEAVE

Type and textiles share many common prototypes, found in the form of woven tapestries and intarsia embroidery, for instance. Time and again thread has been a medium used to capture images and text in elaborate processes and thus honor their significance. This is still the case today, even in popular culture, as evidenced by the soccer fan scarf.

Both typography and textiles have adapted to the work and reproduction techniques of their day and age. Typographical terms like *leading, font,* and *foundry* predate digital design, and remind us of the step-by-step transformation of typographic processes from manual calligraphic copying, through woodcut printing and lead composition, to digital web fonts, with many other stages in between. Automation, and later, digitization, have also had a major impact on the production of textiles, yet at the same time have been influenced by earlier techniques themselves: the punch cards on the first mechanical looms circa 1805 are heralded as an early form of digital coding and marked the beginning of the first industrial revolution. Holes—as an analog counterpart to bytes—became the source code of the weaving industry.

In contrast, little has changed in the stitch design of basic manual knitting techniques. Knit and purl stitches are still used to organize the yarn into its designated shape. And, in its basic form, knitting has always been a binary (digital) system for the manual programming of yarn.

You can generate a QR code with a link to your Instagram account, website, or other texts on *www.goqr.me*. For a large-format throw, knit the pixels as patches [→ p. 127].

KNITTING CIRCLES 2.0

In textile practice, knitting has long been linked to our digital communication channels and social networks. If you want to learn to knit, you can find tutorials on YouTube and Pinterest, on blogs and social media platforms. Physical and virtual strands of yarn seem to attract each other.

As even a purely digital access to this craft requires the use of actual physical materials and as some of the tricks of the trade are better explained in person, any digital excursion frequently leads would-be, and even experienced knitters to real people and places. Knitting is (and always has been) characterized by personal interaction. Yarn stores become *creative hubs*, grandmothers become *technical consultants*, and private knitting circles are platforms where methodological expertise is enthusiastically exchanged.

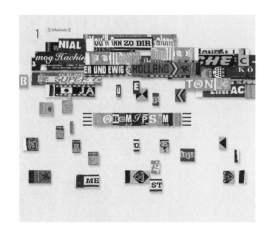

KNITTING AS A JOURNEY

Knitting isn't something you learn at a moment's notice. Just like building up your repertoire in the kitchen by getting to know recipes, it takes time, practice, and an exchange of ideas. Therefore, this book is the result of a number of different projects that I undertook throughout the past years.

In the *Schalalala!* fan scarf remix project (starting during the 2006 World Cup), I developed an interface, together with designer/programmer Jan Lindenberg, in which users could digitally remix original soccer fan scarves. Pixelated fan scarves from private collectors' websites, eBay, and official club stores served as patterns. Originally not a knitter, I initiated a knitting circle to knit up some of the remixes. Here, my knitting repertoire gradually expanded [1, 3].

One result was the *Jönköping Letter Archive*, an online library of letter knitting patterns I developed for the Craftwerk 2.0 exhibition in Jönköping in Sweden in 2009 [2, p.11]. The archive was used for a "crowdknitting" experiment. Physical and virtual visitors knitted single letters that I then knitted together in the order they were submitted [4]. The resulting aleatoric text was enhanced by the multitude of personal knitting techniques brought by the participants.

With *The gnittinK Room* [5], a para-digital workshop held during the *Neue Masche* (New Stitch) exhibition at the Museum Bellerive in Zurich in Switzerland in 2011, I picked up the threads (or yarn) with the *Knit & Type* workshop, which laid the methodical foundations for the this book.

The encounters made during the course of these projects were essential. Horst Schulz, a pioneer of patchwork knitting, whose modular mashup of knitting techniques acted as my incentive for learning to knit, provided the inspiration for the last two chapters of this book. For my project "Conceptual Knitting Circle," numerous participants in Berlin, Kyoto, and Zurich contributed ideas imported from other fields (including electronic music, coding, and weaving) that went well beyond the practical crafting level, and enriched my understanding of the knowledge-generating potential of knitting for designers.

As you will find when you use this book, knitting is an extremely communicative medium that encourages interaction. This is true of both the process of learning and making—there are tips to be found everywhere in everyday life—and to wearing and sharing your finished projects. Who wouldn't be delighted to receive their intials in knitted form? And what kinds of messages can be smuggled into any number of public places with *typeknitting*?!

This book presents you with an open-ended collection of methods to accompany you on your *typeknitting* journey and help you extend the possibilities of knit typography. It will provide you with inspiration for many further projects, in which pixels and stitches, knitting and type, combine to form their very own mixed discipline—*typeknitting!*

Rüdiger Schlömer, Zurich 2018

Typeknitting:
Knitting for Typographers

Designers approach knitting with a different aim than hobby knitters do. They're not looking for sock patterns and patchwork throws but for graphic structures and effects that use the constraints of the medium as a generator of design. They want to reinterpret digital and craft tropes in order to produce surprising visual and structural results.

Before you begin your *typeknitting* adventure, however, you will need to familiarize yourself with the art of knitting. This way you can learn where there's room to play and where its limitations lie, and then devise your own method of working.

INSPIRATION AND INPUT

Knitting cannot be depicted linearly nor in its entirety; the learning process involves a lot of trial and error and is enriched by personal encounters along the way. Yarn stores have always been places where keen knitters converge, seizing the opportunity to swap valuable tips and knowledge. (Incidentally, many yarn stores have a few freelance knitters at hand who will knit your designs for you.)

Lots of yarn stores hold regular knitting circles that are well worth attending. You can see how various techniques are applied, pick up some useful tips, try out the materials, and maybe find some inspiration for your own knitting projects. Even if you're not particularly interested in baby blankets or woolly hats, these items can teach you fundamental knitting techniques that can later be mined in your experiments with *typeknitting* (and which make great practice projects where little time and few materials are involved). You might also decide to set up your own knitting group, providing you with a communicative and motivating forum where you can exchange ideas with other knitters and learn with them.

There are plenty of video tutorials on YouTube and personal websites that can help you hone your individual knitting skills. On Ravelry (www.ravelry.com), the best-known social media knitting and crochet network, you can find a multitude of patterns and designs, many of them free, plus personal project pages and thematic groups where knitters present their own knitting patterns and finished work. Since its founding in 2007, and with over 7.6 million members to date, Ravelry has revolutionized the knitting industry and become an indispensable platform for knitters, designers, and yarn manufacturers.

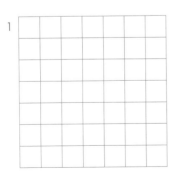

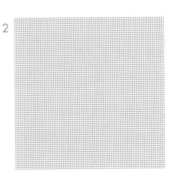

[1] Letter grid for *Print Char 21* (1977), system font *Apple][* [→ p. 188]

[2] Knitting chart for the *Illusion Love Cushion* (2016), knitted with *Illusion Knitting*, Steve Plummer on Ravelry [→ p. 213]

MATERIALS AND TOOLS

Many factors come into play to influence your finished piece of knitting. The main tool alone—the knitting needle—is available in a range of styles: metal, plastic, and bamboo, straight and circular. Depending on which yarn you use, whether the yarn lies securely in your hand or slips, or whether your hands perspire easily and cause some friction with the yarn, will determine which needle may be right for you. Some yarns work best with wooden needles; others work better with metal. And depending on your personal style of knitting, some tools are more practical than others. At first you will only need a few tools to get going.

When buying yarn, look for knitted samples so that you can get a feel for the stitch pattern, size, and structure of the knitted yarn. Multicolored yarns, which look interesting on the ball, may seem very busy on the knitted surface. A yarn that initially looks boring may have just the right rhythm when knitted up.

1   *Circular needles* are especially good for patch-based knitting and simple intarsia work. The cable should be at least 16 in. (40 cm) long.

2   *Crochet hooks* can help you to pick up dropped stitches or add ornamental lines.

3   *Latch hooks* can be used to appliqué lines onto your finished work or to join pieces of a sweater as a test.

4   *Bamboo needles* are suitable for medium-sized stitch- or pattern-based projects and are slightly easier to use, especially when you're beginning to knit.

5   Using a *counting frame* you can read off the ratio of stitches to rows on your 4×4 in. (10×10 cm) swatch and adjust your knitting pattern accordingly. You can also measure the needle gauge with it.

6   *Paper clips* can be used to mark your work so that you can find your place more easily.

7   Use a pair of *embroidery scissors* to cut your yarn instead of breaking it off to avoid pulling the stitches too tight.

8   You can block (i.e., shape and stretch) your knitting by lightly pinning it to a flat, padded surface with *rustproof pins* and covering it with a damp cloth. Leave it to dry in shape.

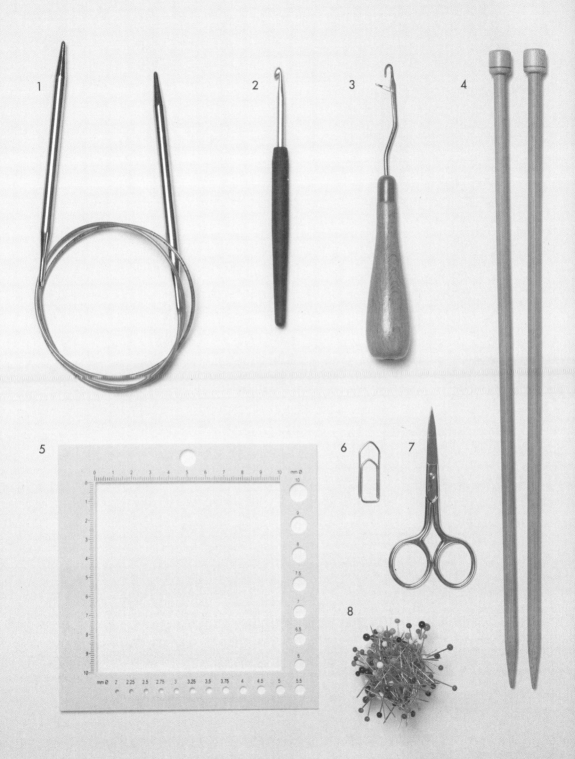

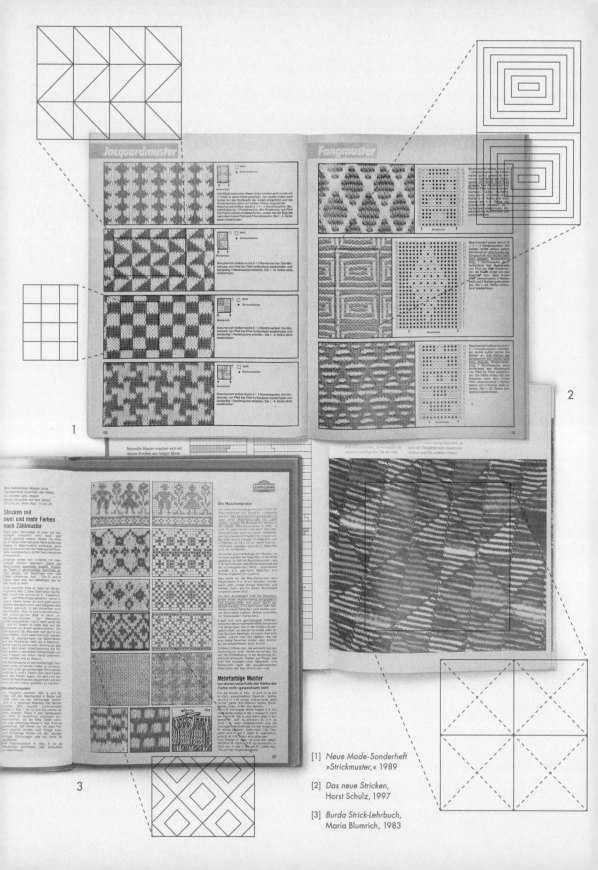

[1] *Neue Mode-Sonderheft*
»Strickmuster,« 1989

[2] *Das neue Stricken,*
Horst Schulz, 1997

[3] *Burda Strick-Lehrbuch,*
Maria Blumrich, 1983

METHODS AND FORMATTING

In both analog and digital design, the designer's methods, tools, and production techniques are implicitly worked into the result. And in that final result, some tools, functions, and programs can be clearly recognized, such as certain image filters in photo retouching, or pitch correction in music production.

When you are knitting type, you experience the influence of method and technique on a very practical level. Unlike embroidery, where you freely apply the thread to the preexisting fabric, knitting produces both the supporting structure and optical surface at once. Knitting techniques, with their various structural characteristics, inherently influence your visual freedom and shape your design in different ways. They also provide you with features you can consciously incorporate into your projects.

Despite knitting's basic and fundamental elements, it offers much room for variation. This is illustrated by the many geographically-specific knitting styles, such as Fair Isle colorwork, Aran cabling, and the highly complex lace knitting patterns developed in Germany by Christine Duchrow. Studying old pattern books from a typographer's perspective can provide inspiration for chart and pattern structures. These can then be compared with existing fonts or taken as a basis for further design.

How to Start *Typeknitting*

The four main chapters in this book are defined by their base elements—*pixels, patterns, patches,* and *modules*—by the corresponding knitting techniques, and thus by the implied rules of design. The examples range from small to large and from simple to advanced. The basic methods I present can be easily combined and expanded, and represent only a small selection of the endless variety of knitting techniques.

Choose where to begin *typeknitting* based on your previous knitting experience. If you've had little or no practice to date, the PIXELS chapter is a good place to start. If you can knit and purl with ease and have mastered simple *intarsia* work, the slip stitches in the PATTERNS section are an easy supplement to your previous skills. With some intarsia and colorwork experience, the PATCHES chapter offers a simple introduction to patchwork knitting, which you can go deeper into in the MODULES section.

Knitting directions

Back and forth

As a patch
(across a corner)

In the round

Wherever you start, take time to try out different techniques. Knit swatches and note the type of yarn, weight, needle size, and time taken; these are important pieces of information for later projects. Switch between manual and digital prototyping and scale up your test patches in Photoshop to make larger designs. Once you've explored the characteristics of the various techniques and yarns somewhat, there's nothing to stop you from starting your first *typeknitting* project!

PIXELS	PATTERNS	PATCHES	MODULES
[→p.88]	[→p.102]	[→p.126]	[→p.138]

TEXTURE

When knitting type, your result is largely determined by the stitch pattern. One pixel on the template is knitted to form a V-shaped stitch. This stitch is not square as on the chart but slightly oblong, depending on the materials and the way you knit, and has an aspect ratio 2:3 or 3:4, for example.

To compensate for this, with small knitted fonts, you can knit in extra pixels (1 pixel = 1 stitch). The larger you knit the letter, the more easily you can adjust the number of stitches that make up each pixel (for example, 1 pixel = 5 stitches × 6 rows) [→p. 88].

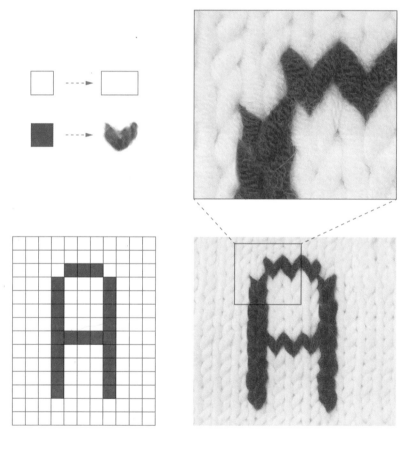

TYPE PATTERNS

The easiest way to create your own knitting patterns is to print out your templates with intense pixelation. First reduce the pattern down to the required size (40 × 40 stitches = 40 × 40 pixels). Then make a large-format print. You can also make physical templates by tracing your design onto graph paper.

To compensate for the stitch shape, you can adjust the ratio of stitches to pixels in your template. You can create graph paper with the right stitch ratio in Excel or with free tools available online [→ p. 212].

You can create templates from images of type samples using online editors, such as Pixlr [→ p. 212].

If you want to make a one-to-one knitting pattern for a classic typeface, details such as serifs or counters are quickly lost or become misshapen, especially in smaller formats. You should therefore try out various sizes on a test patch, or knit up a swatch.

Bodoni

Giddyup

Clarendon Bold

Bauhaus

Helvetica

Times New Roman

Thirsty Rough

Futura

Gill Sans Ultra Bold

KNITTING DIRECTION

Depending on which direction you knit your pattern in, the V-shaped stitches point up or down, to the left or to the right. At an angle of 45 degrees, the stitch shape either forms a jagged edge or merges into the diagonal.

If the cast-on row is along the lower or upper edge, the baseline is jagged and the vertical elements are straight [1, 3]. If you cast on along the left or right edge, the baseline is straight [2, 4].

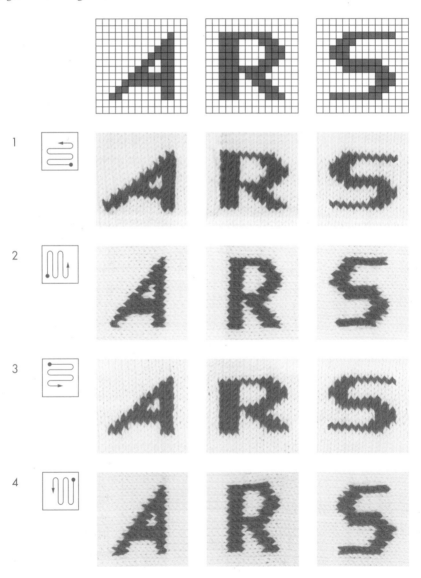

PERSONAL STYLE

Knitting, as an activity, is inextricably linked to the body. Implicit factors, such as rhythm, the way you hold your hands, and how you sit will mold your individual style almost as strongly as your choice of color and materials. Your stitch texture is your "signature."

Your personal style starts to manifest itself with the preparation of the knitting pattern: you can meticulously knit up a pixel diagram with dithering pixel for pixel (or stitch by stitch) or geometrically adapt it to suit the knitting pattern chart.

When exploring new techniques, always allow yourself to learn "backward." What may have been a mistake can be incorpo-rated as a conscious element of your own style: flashes of color showing through from the back of intarsia work, (il)legibility of pixelated patterns, a mixture of dissimilar types of yarn, stranded yarn on the back of your work. Asking someone else for their opinion—at your knitting circle or on an online forum, for example—often helps you to view your own efforts more objectively.

And as with all tests: don't be discouraged if a design doesn't immediately work out as planned and you must start again. Be patient with yourself, and with your yarn. Your next attempt will be easier—and it's all worth it in the end!

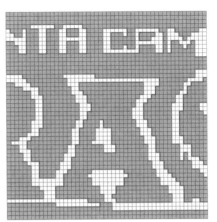

Pixel template (height: 50 px)

Final artwork (in two colors)

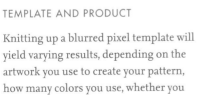

TEMPLATE AND PRODUCT

Knitting up a blurred pixel template will yield varying results, depending on the artwork you use to create your pattern, how many colors you use, whether you translate the template pixel by pixel or simply straighten it, and the direction you knit in.

COLLABORATIVE PROJECTS

For new knitting circles, collaborations make good initial projects. The *Patchmatch* remix fan scarf is based on scarf patterns from FC Bayern Munich, Japan, FC Schalke 04, Brazil, FC Cologne, and other soccer teams. It was remixed by Horst Schulz and knitted together with Christel Artz, Monika Faul, Kerstin Hering, Renate Korpus, and Eveline Riefer-Rucht.

THE FIVE
BOXING
WIZARDS
JUMP
QUICKLY
THE FIVE
BOXING

Typeknitting Workshop
Burg Giebichenstein, Halle

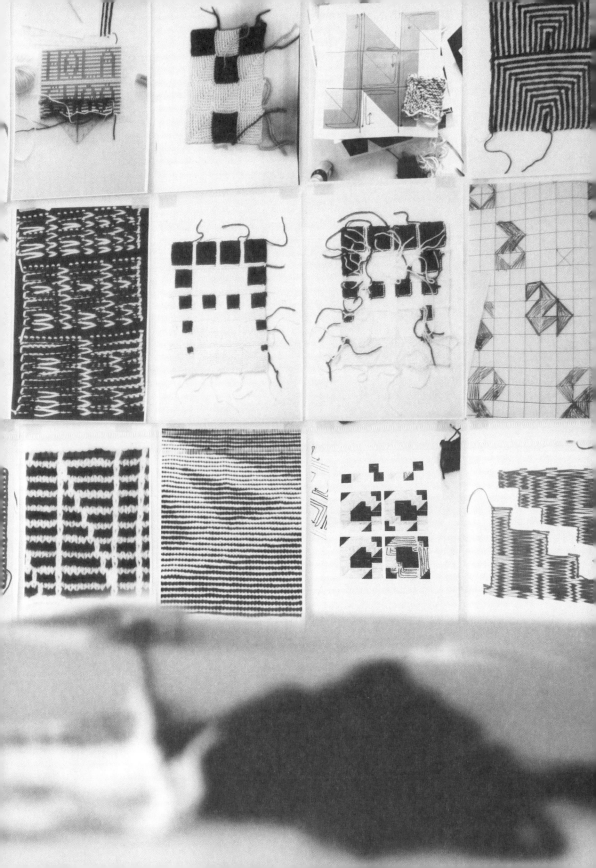

Prototyping session

FONT: OBLONG, LO-RES [→PP. 200–201]
TECHNIQUE: FAIR ISLE [→P. 92]
OBJECT: CUSHION [→P. 162]

FONT: PRINT CHAR 21, LO-RES [→PP. 188, 201]
TECHNIQUE: FAIR ISLE [→P. 92]
OBJECT: SWATCH

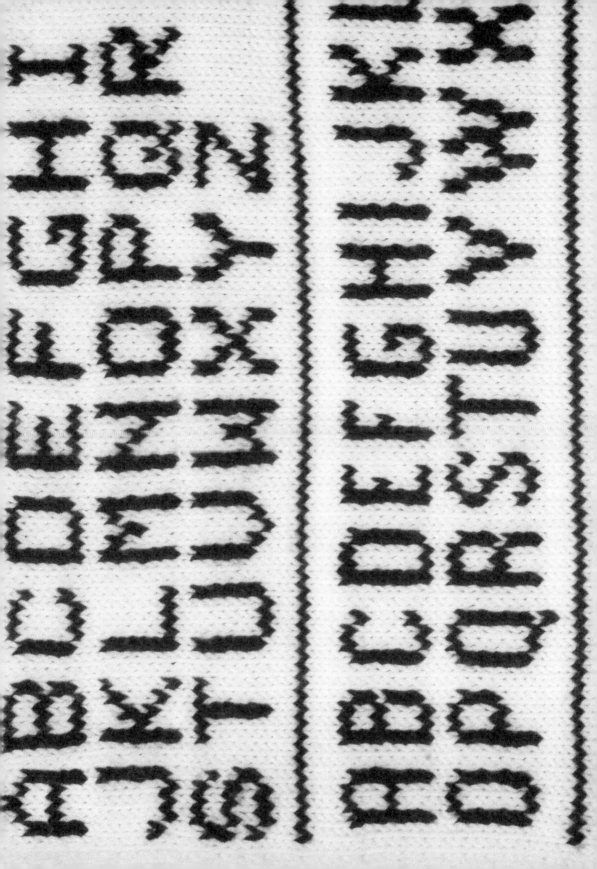

FONT: LŸNO (KARL NAWROT & RADIM PESKO) [→P. 212]
TECHNIQUE: ILLUSION KNITTING [→PP. 109, 174]
OBJECT: ILLUSION KNITTING BLANKET [→P. 174]

FONT: ELEMENTAR SANS [→ PP. 193–195]
TECHNIQUE: FAIR ISLE [→ P. 92]
OBJECT: PROTOTYPE

FONT: HELVETICA (SCREENSHOT) [→ P. 162]
TECHNIQUE: GRAYSCALING WITH
KNITTING PATTERNS [→ P. 100]
OBJECT: PROTOTYPE

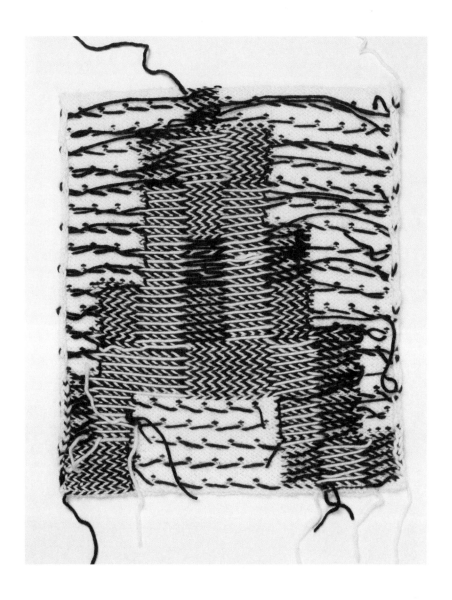

FONT: HELVETICA (SCREENSHOT) [→P. 162]
TECHNIQUE: GRAYSCALING WITH
KNITTING PATTERNS (BACK) [→P. 100]
OBJECT: PROTOTYPE

FONT: ELEMENTAR SANS [→PP. 193–195]
TECHNIQUE: FAIR ISLE (BACK) [→P. 92]
OBJECT: PROTOTYPE

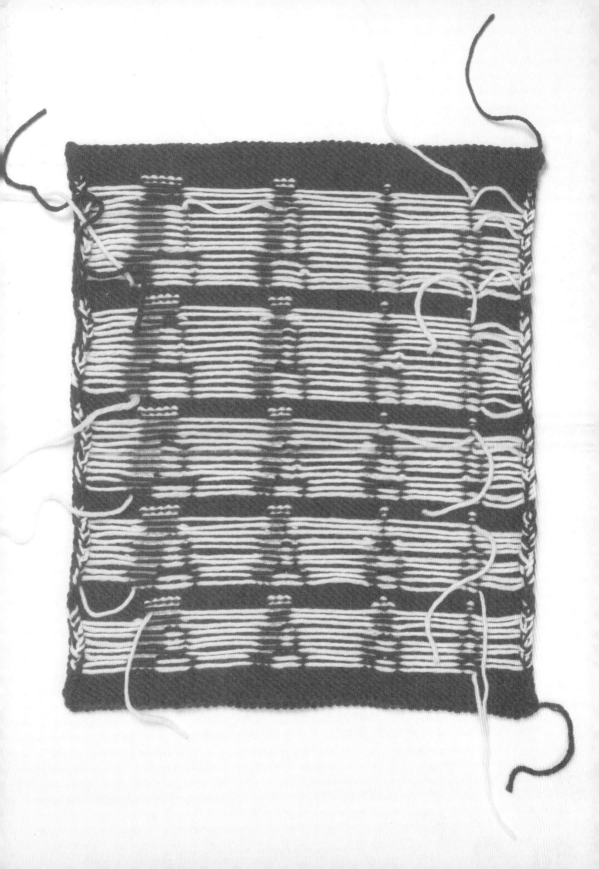

FONT: LO-RES [→P. 201]
TECHNIQUE: FAIR ISLE [→P. 92]
OBJECT: PROTOTYPE

FONT: MONTEREY [→P. 189]
TECHNIQUE: SLIP STITCHES AS A GRID [→P. 116]
OBJECT: PROTOTYPE

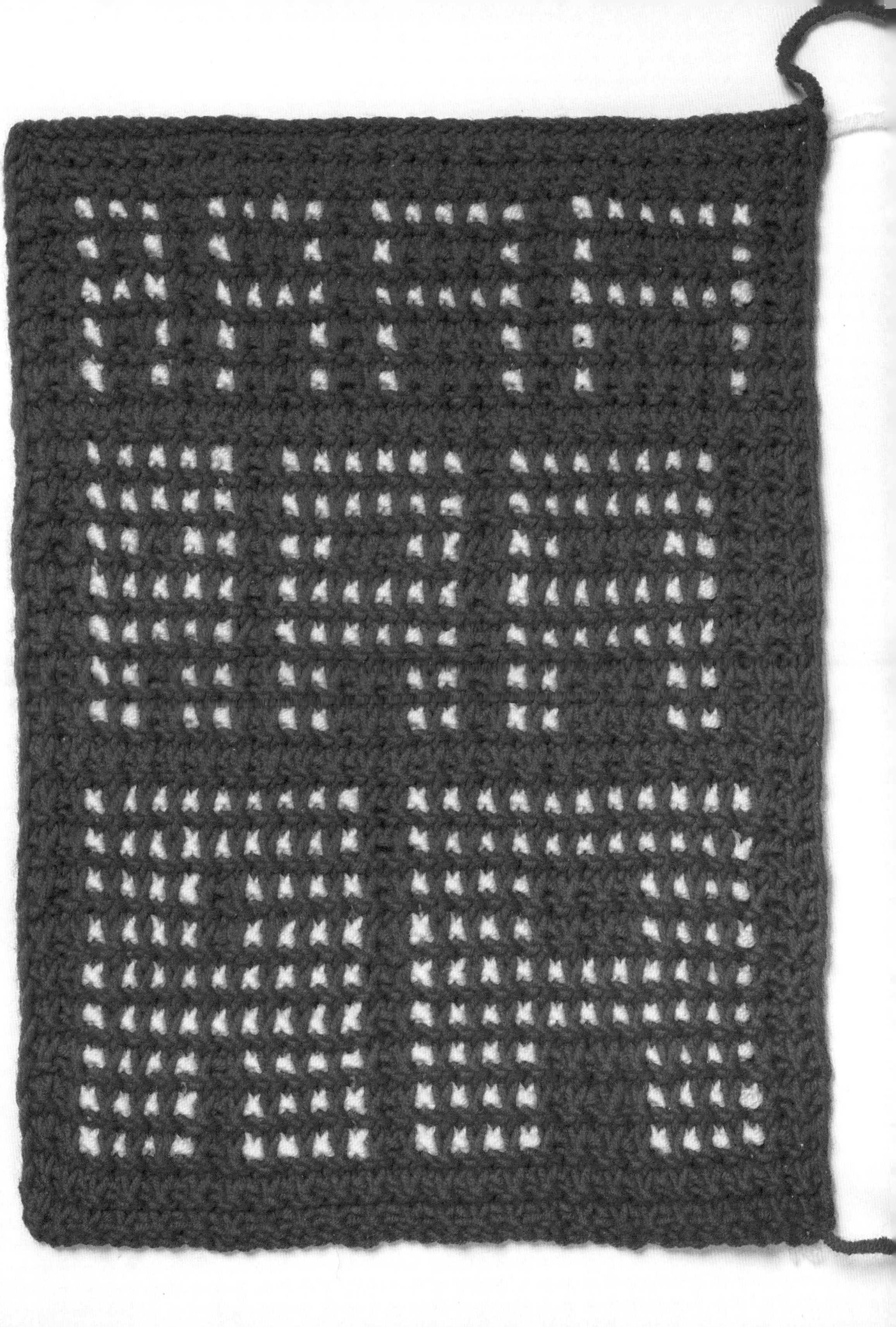

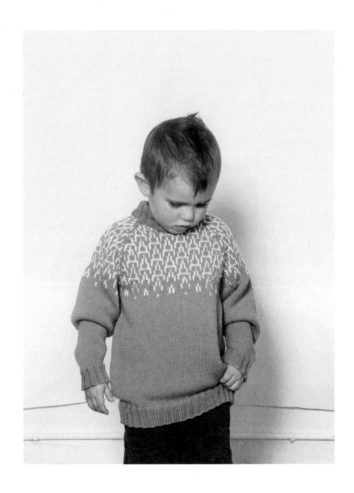

FONT: ELEMENTAR SANS B [→P.195]
TECHNIQUE: FAIR ISLE [→P.92]
OBJECT: CHILD'S FAIR ISLE SWEATER [→P.185]

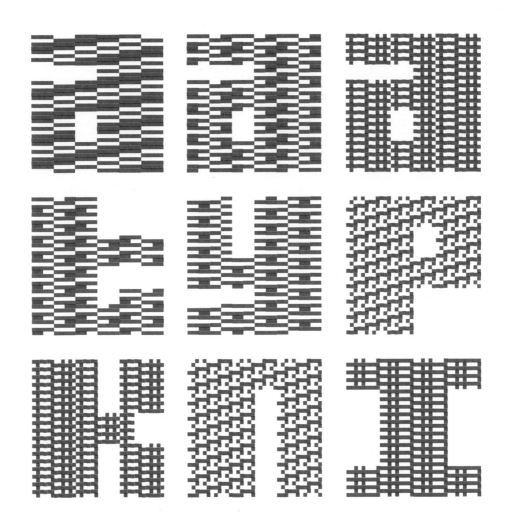

FONT: TYPEJOCKEY KNIT [→PP.120–125]
TECHNIQUE: FAIR ISLE [→P.92]
OBJECT: PROTOTYPE

FONT: FAN SCARF ELEMENTS
TECHNIQUE: INTARSIA [→P. 92]
OBJECT: REMIX FAN SCARF [→P.164]

FONT: LO-RES [→ P. 201]
TECHNIQUE: FAIR ISLE [→ P. 92]
OBJECT: PROTOTYPE

FONT: MODUL CORNER KNIT [→ P. 148]
TECHNIQUE: CORNER PATCH MODULE [→ P. 140]
OBJECT: PROTOTYPE

FONT: IN PROGRESS (FLORE LEVROUW)
TECHNIQUE: DIAGONAL CORNER PATCH [→ P. 152]
OBJECT: PROTOTYPE

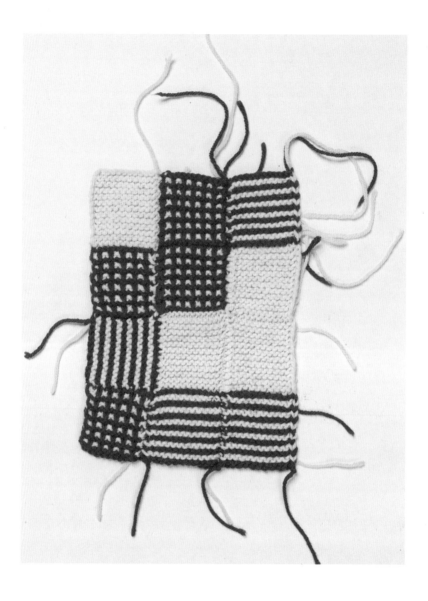

FONT: CUSTOM
TECHNIQUE: SLIP STITCHES AS A GRID [→P.116]
OBJECT: PROTOTYPE

FONT: CUSTOM
TECHNIQUE: SLIP STITCHES AS LINES [→P.112]
OBJECT: PROTOTYPE

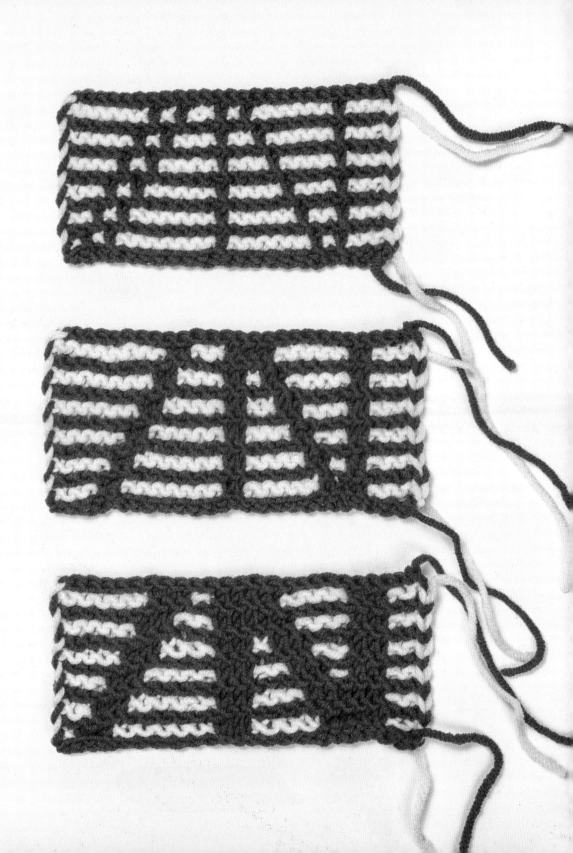

FONT: CUSTOM
TECHNIQUE: SLIP STITCHES AS LINES [→P.112]
OBJECT: SLIP-STITCH SWEATER [→P.178]

FONT: GEM DESKTOP 2.0 [→P.192]
TECHNIQUE: FAIR ISLE, KNITTED IN THE ROUND [→P.92]
OBJECT: SELBU MITTENS [→P.170]

FONT: ELEMENTAR SANS B [→ P.193]
TECHNIQUE: INTARSIA, STOCKINETTE STITCH [→ P. 92]
OBJECT: CHILD'S INTARSIA SWEATER [→ P.182]

FONT: ELEMENTAR [→ PP. 193–195]
TECHNIQUE: DOUBLE-FACE [→ P. 93]
OBJECT: DOUBLE-FACE HAT [→ P. 166]

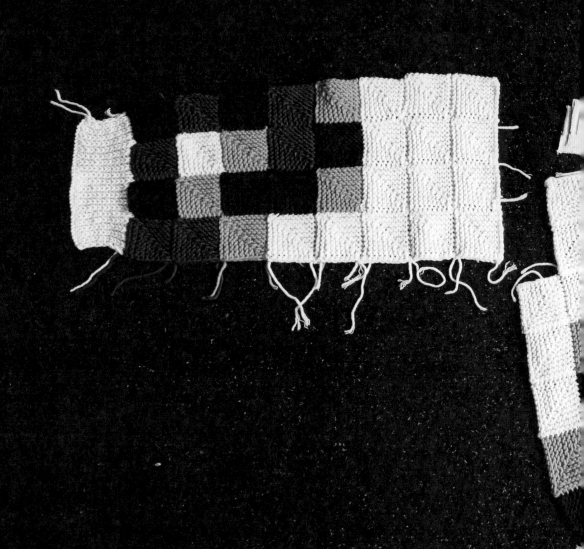

FONT: HELVETICA (SCREENSHOT) [→P.136]
TECHNIQUE: CORNER PATCH [→P.128]
OBJECT: PATCHWORK SWEATER [→P.176]

FONT: CALCULA [→P.198]
TECHNIQUE: SLIP STITCHES AS A GRID [→P.116]
OBJECT: CHILD'S SLIP-STITCH SWEATER [→P.184]

GLYPH: ALDUS LEAF
TECHNIQUE: FAIR ISLE [→ P. 92]
OBJECT: PROTOTYPE

I.

KNITTING BASICS

Basic techniques

There are many different ways of learning to knit: at a workshop, from a knitting book, by watching video tutorials, or from someone who shows you in person, such as at an intergenerational knitting circle. You can find useful tips and techniques in all sorts of places and they will all help you to gradually develop your own personal style of knitting. The following pages contain a summary of some of the basic principles that have proved helpful when knitting type.

STARTING OUT

Knitting is a compilation of numerous combined hand movements. Each one is relatively easy to understand and learn. Only when these basic techniques are combined does the process become more complex. Don't be discouraged by advanced projects!

Everyone has to find their own way of starting out and learning. However, the range of projects available has never been so vast. Would-be knitters can follow a whole host of printed and digital instructions and video tutorials [→ p. 213], visit local workshops, and pore over knitting books both old and new.

There's no "correct" way of holding and tensioning the yarn. Ask experienced knitters for practical tips and which guides and patterns work best for them and why. Some questions only arise while you're actually knitting; others soon sort themselves out. Work forward step by step, and set your own knitting speed.

You can treat the knitting structure as a referential weave: knitting is basically a stitch made from a stitch made from a stitch. It all starts with a cast-on loop.

Place your finger on the yarn.

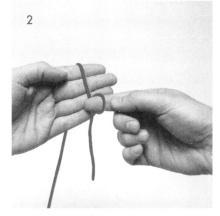

Wrap it around your finger.

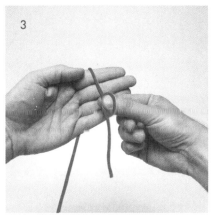

Reach through and pick up the yarn.

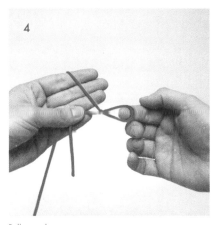

Pull out a loop.

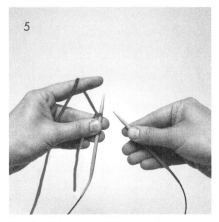

Place the slip knot on the left-hand needle.

CASTING ON

Use a *knit cast-on* ("knitting on") so that later you can easily pick up and knit stitches from the lower edge. First, place the slip knot on the left-hand needle. Knit a stitch from this loop [1–3] and twist it around back onto the left-hand needle [4]. If you leave your needle in the stitch you've just made, the needle is in the right place to make the next stitch and the yarn isn't pulled too tight [5]. Repeat this process until you have the right number of stitches on your left-hand needle. If you're counting in double rows for pattern- or patch-based knitting, this cast-on row counts as the first right-side row.

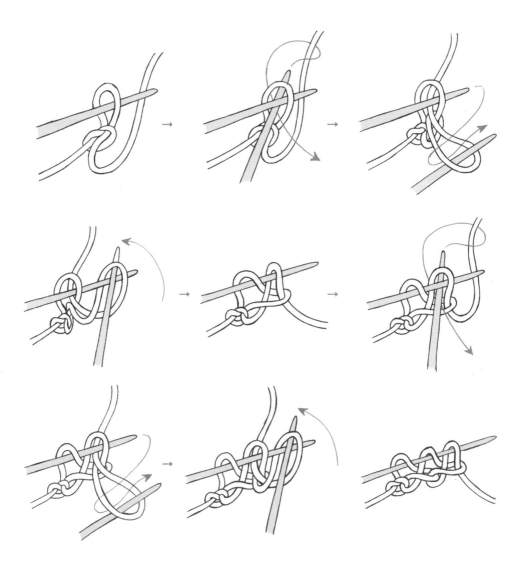

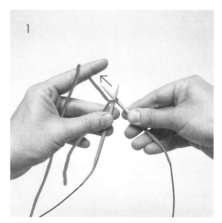

Insert the right-hand needle into the loop.

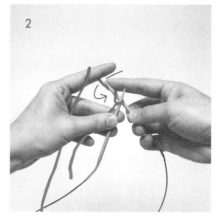

Knit a stitch from the loop.

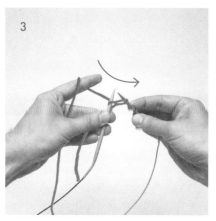

Pull the yarn out in a wide loop.

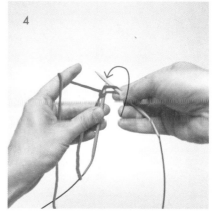

Twist the stitch back onto the left-hand needle.

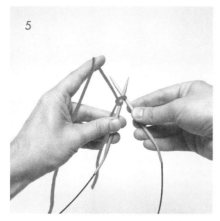

Leave the needle in the stitch and pull the stitch tight.

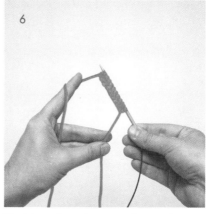

Check the number and evenness of your stitches.

KNIT STITCHES

If you're right-handed, you knit right to left and not in the direction we read. To make knit stitches, you insert your needle into the next stitch from front to back and pull out a stitch to the front. You then slide the stitch off the left-hand needle.

PURL STITCHES

When making purl stitches, you insert your needle into the next stitch from back to front and pull the yarn through to the back. You then slide the stitch off the left-hand needle. Purl stitches look like the wrong side of knit stitches.

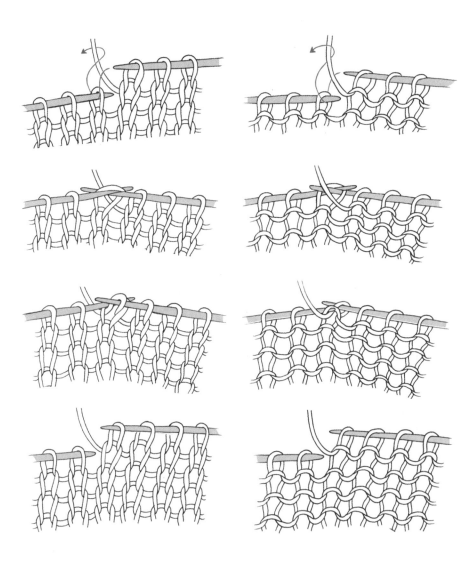

COMBINATIONS

By combining knit and purl stitches in right- and wrong-side rows you can make various patterns and structures. In the PIXEL chapter, you always knit in stockinette stitch (knit all right-side rows, purl all wrong-side rows) [1]. One row of pixels equals one row of stitches. If you knit with two colors of yarn at the same time, you achieve a random pattern [2].

In the PATCH chapter, you use garter stitch [3] (knit all rows); in the PATTERN and MODULE chapters, you knit in several colors in garter stitch [3] or alternate between garter stitch and stockinette stitch [4]. In all three of the above chapters, one row of pixels counts as a double row (a right-side plus a wrong-side row).

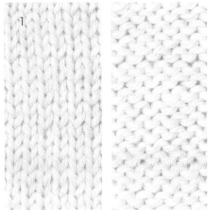

Stockinette stitch   (back)

Stockinette stitch knit with two strands of different-colored yarn

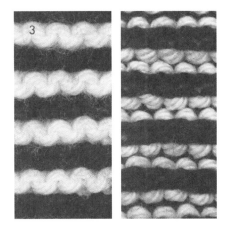

Garter stitch in two alternate colors
(per double row)

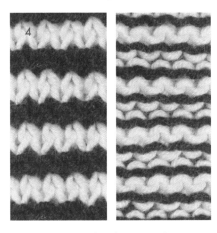

Alternating garter/stockinette stitch in two alternate colors (per double row)

BASIC PATCHWORK KNITTING

When knitting type, you'll make use of a few basic patchwork knitting principles. These only become fundamental to the construction of the individual letters in the PATCH and MODULE chapters. Though it's also worth adopting these principles in the PIXEL and PATTERN chapters; they allow you to easily knit the individual components together at a later stage.

In essence, patchwork knitting is modular. Instead of knitting each patch or mitred square separately and then laboriously piecing them together, you join them as you knit. This means that the edge stitches on all sides must be wide enough for you to pick up and, from them, knit the edge stitches for the next patch or letter.

It's a good idea to practice these basic principles on a few sample patches before you embark on a larger project. You'll also find suitable video tutorials online [→ p. 213], or courses on offer at specialist wool stores.

So that you can easily knit onto all four sides of a patch at a later stage, use the following basic principles:

Use a *knit cast-on* so that you can also pick up and knit stitches along the lower edge. In double rows, this cast-on row counts as the first right-side row [→ p. 76].

Edge stitches always apply to two rows (a double row). This makes the edge stitches big enough for new stitches to be made from them. To this end, slide the last stitch on each row (right- and wrong-side rows) onto the right-hand needle without knitting a stitch [→ p. 82].

Bind off work knitted back and forth in rows (PIXEL and PATTERN chapters) in the usual manner on the last wrong-side row. To do so, knit two stitches and pass the first stitch over the second. Repeat this to the end of the row [→ p. 87].

In the PATCH chapter, your knitting doesn't have to be bound off as only one stitch is left at the end of the patch. In the MODULE chapter, you only bind off those edges that can't be finished in any other way [→ p. 147].

KNITTING A PATCH

The cast-on row counts as the first right-side row. On the wrong-side row, insert your needle from front to back into the first stitch and knit to the end of the row.

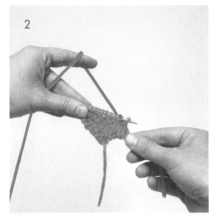

After knitting about a third of it, your patch starts to take on its final shape.

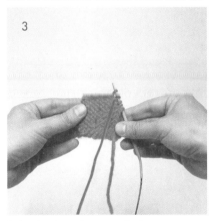

Each right-side row has two stitches less.

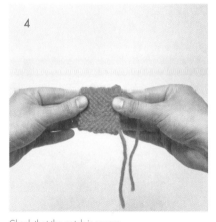

Check that the patch is square.

The patch takes on its square shape by knitting the three center stitches together on all wrong-side rows [5]. This means that two stitches are reduced in each double row and the patch gradually becomes a square. [→ p.128]

EDGE STITCHES

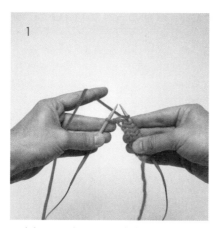

Work the row in the pattern to the last stitch but one.

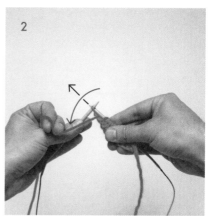

Bring the yarn to the front and insert your needle into the last stitch.

Slide the last stitch onto the right-hand needle without knitting it.

Check the number and evenness of your stitches.

Always knit edge stitches across a double row. To this end, slide the last stitch on each right- and wrong-side row onto the right-hand needle without knitting it. If you then continue to knit, bring the yarn to the front before you do so [2]. This makes the edge stitches big enough for new stitches to be made from them [5].

Picking up and knitting from an edge stitch.

PICKING UP FROM EDGE STITCHES

Hold patch 1 in your left hand in the knitting direction (the cast-on strand of yarn is on the bottom right, with the bind off on the top right).

Insert your needle into the first stitch.

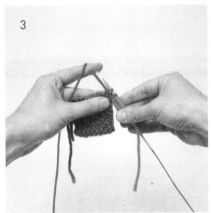

Move the yarn to the back of your work and knit a stitch.

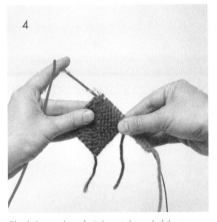

Check the number of stitches at the end of the row.

To pick up and knit stitches from edge stitches, hold the patch in your left hand and your needle in the right [1]. To start with, the edge stitches at the corners are difficult to recognize. Therefore, count them so that you don't miss any. Then insert your needle into the first edge stitch [2] and loop the yarn from back to front like you would for a knit stitch [3]. Repeat this until there are as many knit stitches on your needle as there are edge stitches on the left-hand patch. You can then knit the next patch as normal.

ADDING A PATCH ON THE RIGHT

After picking up and knitting stitches from the edge of patch 1, continue with patch 2.

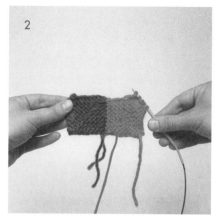

Always knit the three center stitches together on a wrong-side row.

After knitting the last three stitches together, draw the yarn through the remaining stitch.

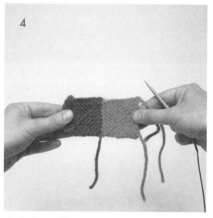

Check that neighboring patches are of identical height.

To add a neighboring patch to the right of an existing patch, hold patch 1 in front of you in the knitting direction. Cast on the first row of patch 2 as usual, stopping in the middle of the row. From here pick up and knit the rest of the row from the edge stitches along the side of patch 1 [1].

Complete the patch as usual, always knitting the three center stitches together on each wrong-side row [2 – 4].

ADDING A PATCH TO THE TOP

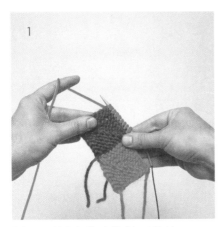

Pick up and knit the first half of the right-side row of patch 3 from the top edge of patch 1.

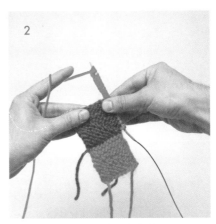

Cast on the remaining stitches for the first row of patch 3.

Continue patch 3 in pattern, always knitting the three center stitches together on a wrong-side row.

Check that neighboring patches are of identical height.

For patch 3, which you knit onto the top of patch 1, you do the opposite. First, you pick up and knit stitches from the top edge of patch 1 [1]. Cast on stitches as usual for the second half of the first row of patch 3 [2]. Then complete the patch in pattern as usual [3 – 4].

The procedure for patch 4 is the same as for patch 2. As patch 5 is joined to existing patches on both sides, pick up and knit the entire first row from the edges of patches 2 and 3. Patch 6 is the same as for patch 3.

SLIP STITCHES

With the yarn at the back on a right-side row, insert your needle into the next stitch.

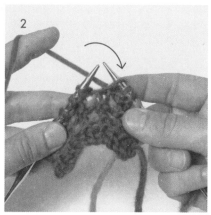

Slide this onto the right-hand needle without knitting it and then knit a stitch.

On a wrong-side row, insert your needle into the next stitch with the yarn in front.

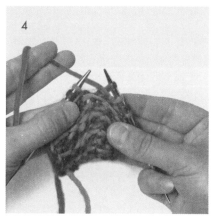

Slip this onto the right-hand needle without knitting it, move the yarn to the back, and then knit a stitch.

To make slip stitches you simply slide the stitch onto the right-hand needle without knitting it [1–2]. The unknitted yarn is loosely carried along the back of your work.

To make a slip stitch on a wrong-side row, hold the unknitted yarn in front of your work [3] (otherwise it later shows in front of the slipped stitch) and slide the stitch onto the right-hand needle. For the next knit stitch, you again move the yarn to the back of your work [4].

KNITTING PIECES TOGETHER

To join two finished pieces of knitting, pick up and knit a row from the stitches along both edges using a circular needle [1–2]. Keep the yarn between the two pieces as short as possible. Then place the two knitted letters exactly on top of one another, aligning the picked-up stitches along the edges [3].

Using a third needle, knit two picked-up stitches (one of each letter) together [4]. Knit the pieces together as you would for a normal bind-off: once you have made two stitches, pass the first stitch over the second [8–9]. Repeat until you have knitted the last stitch. Depending on whether you bind off with both *right-* or *wrong-sides* facing, the bind-off is on the front or back of your work.

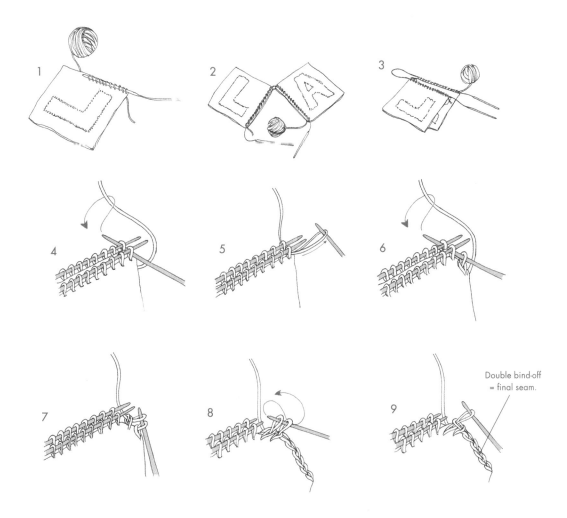

Double bind-off = final seam.

II.

PIXELS

Pixel fonts with intarsia,
Fair Isle, or double-face knitting
in one or more colors

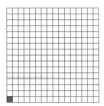

Stitch-based knitting is the easiest and most basic way of knitting type; the stitch design will have a strong visual dominance. Pixel fonts take on a noisy, post-digital character when they are translated into intarsia designs that are knit in one or more colors.

TWO-COLOR DESIGNS

When knitting stockinette stitch, it's very simple to work in color changes. To add a second color, you simply discard yarn 1 and continue in yarn 2. To make things easier you can loosely tie yarn 2 to yarn 1 before you start. When knitting small-format letters, make sure that the stitch has a basic square shape [→ p. 20].

In order to obtain a feel for the finished piece of knitting, it's useful to knit an intarsia swatch with various aspect ratios. In theory, intarsia patterns can be knitted with unlimited colors of yarn. The more yarns you use, however, the quicker you're likely to end up in a tangle of knots!

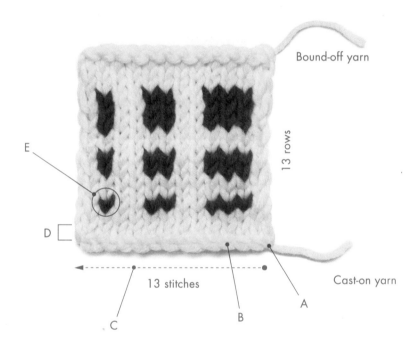

A	Cast-on loop
B	Cast-on row
C	Knitting direction
D	Edge stitch for rows 1 and 2
E	Intarsia motif in color 2

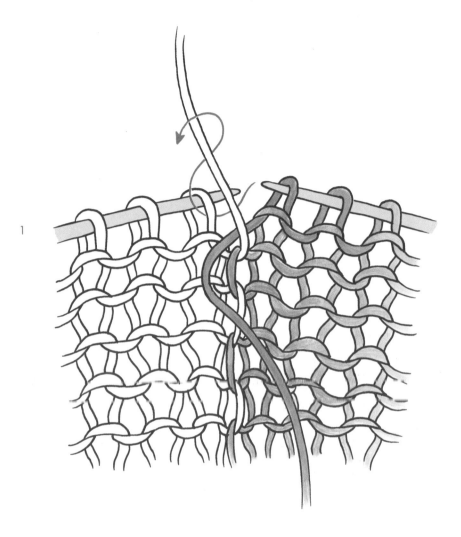

CHANGING COLORS

To change color on a knit row, place yarn 2 at the back of your work and loosely knot it onto yarn 1. This is a big taboo for experienced knitters but can help when you're just starting out. Leave a loose end about 1.5 in. (4 cm) long so that you can pull it tight later. On a wrong-side row of purl stitches, place the new yarn in front of your work [1].

When changing color, always twist the yarns together, otherwise a poncho-like hole appears. Also make sure to keep the stranded yarns loose or your work will pucker.

BACKS

Yarn can be carried along the back of your knitting in different ways depending on the pattern to make your work easier. In the Fair Isle technique, the yarn is stranded across the wrong side of your knitting. On larger pieces of *intarsia*, you avoid stranding by working with several different balls of yarn. This means that the finished piece is thinner and you use up less wool.

There are also two advanced methods for enhanced colorwork backsides: one is *weaving*, where the unused color is woven into the back of your work. This gives you an interesting design, which, if knitted up in a regular pattern, can also be used as the front. The other is double-face knitting, where stranding is completely avoided by knitting an inverted motif on the back.

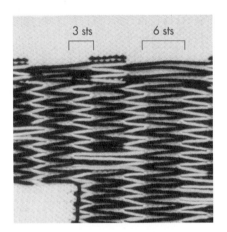

STRANDING: FAIR ISLE

If in colorwork you strand or float the yarn not in use across the back of your work [1], it is carried to the next stitch in that color. This isn't a problem with cushions; with sweaters, no more than five stitches should be stranded, otherwise you'll get tangled in your knitting! Make sure to hold stranded yarn loosely or your knitting will pucker.

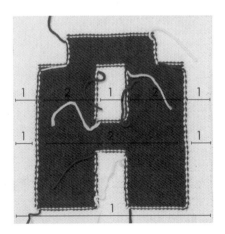

AVOIDING STRANDING: INTARSIA

To avoid stranding, you can use one ball of wool per section of color [2]. This is better for large-format motifs, but it also depends on the letter. For an *A*, you'll need up to three balls of color 1 and two balls of color 2. For a letter with more vertical stems, such as an *M*, you'll need five balls of color 1 and four of color 2.

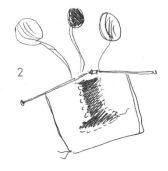
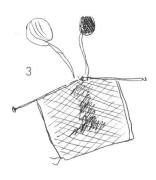

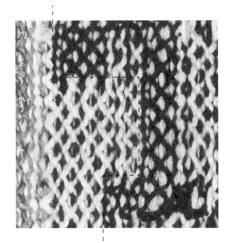

WEAVING

To weave in strands on the wrong side of
your work [3], you place the unused yarn
alternately to the front and the back of the
needle when picking up stitches. Thus a
diagonal grid pattern is formed on the
wrong side, with the woven yarn showing
through the gaps. This makes your
knitting thicker and stronger. Depending
on your accuracy the woven back can also
be used as the front.

Right side   Wrong side

INVERTED BACKS: DOUBLE FACE

In regular double-face knitting, you knit
your motif in parallel in two colors, once
on the front and once on the back. If the
letter on the front is light on a dark
background, it will be the exact reverse on
the back. This makes the finished work
twice as thick but gives you a mirror image
on both sides. (More advanced knitters can
try knitting double-face with different
motifs on front and back.)

MODIFYING PIXEL FONTS

If you wish to achieve a specific aspect ratio, such as for hats [→ p. 166] or for the Selbu mittens [→ p. 170], existing pixel fonts can be easily adapted. The same elements that some people consider sacrilege in typography are the same elements that can be used to your advantage in knitting: distortion, irregular modification, and cut and paste.

You can scale the height and width evenly or irregularly, in whole or in part; you can create repeat patterns or take a letter as the basis for an ornamental graphic. This way your letter becomes more and more of a pattern or secret code.

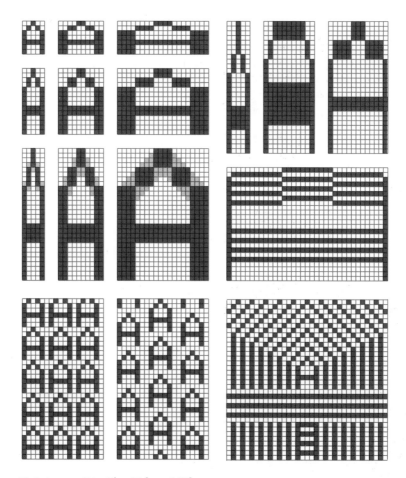

Variations on *Print Char 21* [→ p. 188]

FONT: KK FIXED 4×5 [→P. 132]
TECHNIQUE: FAIR ISLE, STOCKINETTE STITCH [→P. 92]

OUTLINES AND SHADED EDGES

Additional elements, such as accented lines or shaded edges, can also be worked onto the finished piece of knitting. So that these blend in perfectly with the stitch pattern, the wool is embroidered onto the curved line of the yarn with a blunt needle in embroidery stitch. You can also chain stitch lines onto your knitting using a crochet or latch hook.

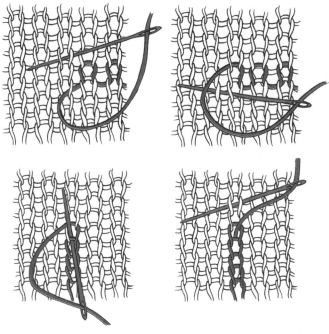

EMBROIDERED LETTERS

With a little effort, you can also embroider entire letters onto knitted clothing. Cut out a paper pattern and place this on the knitting. Sew on the outline using a sewing thread that forms a good contrast with the background. Embroider the inside of the letter first and then the outline. You can use a stem stitch, a chain stitch, or a crocheted line of slip stitches.

FONT: LO-RES 9 NARROW BOLD (EMIGRE) [→ P. 212]
TECHNIQUE: INTARSIA, STOCKINETTE STITCH [→ P. 92], EMBROIDERY STITCH

SCALING UP BY COMBINING YARNS

To scale up your *typeknitting* project, you can simply increase the number of yarns used and knit with bigger needles. This is very useful if you want to combine different types of yarn, use up your scrap wool, or merge different textures.

Depending on the number of yarns used, your knitted piece may be thicker, which is good for winter sweaters, cushions, and blankets. If you want to achieve a multicolored effect for finer items, simply use thinner yarn.

1 yarn
4.5-mm (US/UK 7) needles

2 yarns
7-mm (US 10.5/UK 2) needles

3 yarns
9-mm (US 13/UK 00) needles

ADAPTING THE KNITTING CHART

In order to adapt a pixel font to a knitting chart, you can calculate the aspect ratio using a swatch measuring 4×4 in. (10×10 cm). A swatch 20 stitches wide and 30 rows high has an aspect ratio of 2:3. To compensate for this, you must scale up your template vertically by 150 percent.

To optically adjust a letter directly, you can sketch onto a tracing paper or transparent file jackets placed over the swatch.

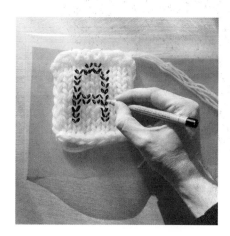

FONT: GEM DESKTOP 2.0 [→P. 192]
TECHNIQUE: FAIR ISLE, STOCKINETTE STITCH [→P. 92]

GRAYSCALING WITH KNITTING PATTERNS

You can scale a pixel template with *anti-aliasing* (the smoothing of edges by adding grayscale pixels) by translating the individual pixels into areas with different patterns.

To do so, draw up patterns with appropriate levels of brightness and allocate these patterns to the grayscaling on your template. Make sure that the stranded yarns between the dots of color are not carried across more than five stitches; otherwise, you will get tangled in your knitting. You can ignore this when knitting cushion covers as the stranded yarns later disappear.

You can knit up test segments in squares of 9×9 stitches, yet the result will be slightly wider than it is high. To adjust the aspect ratio, first knit a swatch and then adapt the template (for example, one segment = 10 stitches × 14 rows). The pattern repeat within the segments stays the same.

If you find it too complicated to knit such fine patterns on a stitch-by-stitch basis, you can also knit up the same pixel template using patches [→ p. 136].

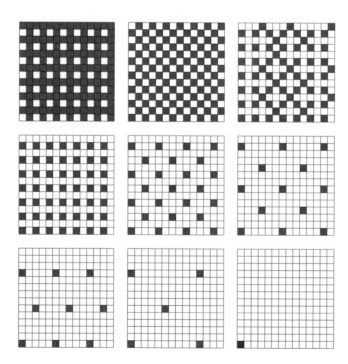

FONT: HELVETICA 8 PT
(SCREENSHOT) [→ P. 162]

III.

PATTERNS

Basic patterned charts
for constructed and dot matrix fonts
with colorwork and slipped stitches

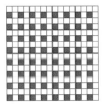

Pattern-based knitting is especially suitable for knitted
objects featuring both small- and large-format letters,
which will have an impact from a distance. Through the
specific use of various color combinations, you can generate numerous visual effects and at the same time give
your work a succinct feel.

DIAGONAL STRIPE

Diagonal stripe is a vertical knitted pattern that you can use to easily create a diagonal design grid. Knit an odd number of rows of two, alternating between garter stitch and stockinette stitch. Roughly speaking, a base area of 13 stitches × 13 rows of two (26 rows of knitting) produces a square.

Use three colors: the odd double rows (1, 3, and 5, etc.) are knitted in garter stitch and color 1 throughout. The even double rows (2, 4, and 6, etc.) are worked in stockinette stitch, alternating between colors 2 and 3.

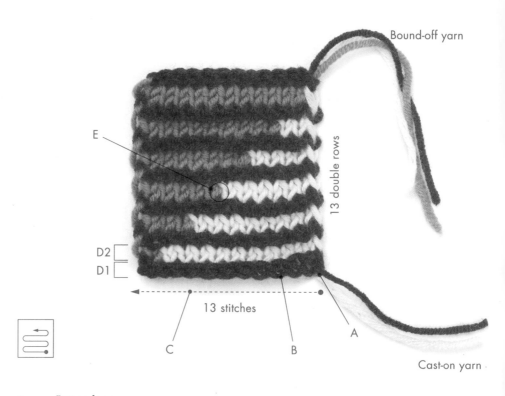

Bound-off yarn

E

13 double rows

D2

D1

13 stitches

C   B   A

Cast-on yarn

A	Cast-on loop
B	Cast-on row
C	Knitting direction
D1	Edge stitch for double row 1 (garter stitch)
D2	Edge stitch for double row 2 (stockinette stitch)
E	Change from color 2 to color 3

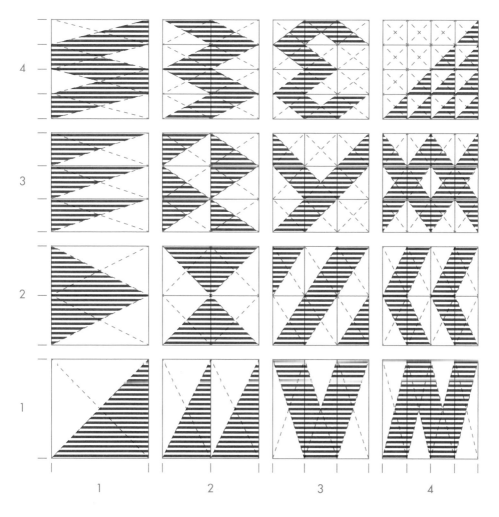

CHART VARIANTS

You obtain a design grid for the diagonals by dividing the stitch format up into horizontal and vertical sections. One advantage of diagonals is that you don't have to keep counting stitches since the increase is regular. You can of course also knit round or free-form shapes with a bit more counting.

KNITTING CHARTS AND DESIGN GRIDS

For a diagonal stripe, use three colors: color 1 forms a grid that is knitted throughout on all odd double rows. Colors 2 and 3 form the actual letter on all even double rows. All odd double rows are knitted in garter stitch and all even rows in stockinette stitch, making the grid stand out and creating an additional haptic effect with shading.

When choosing the knitting chart, select a format that gives you enough scope when designing your letters. If your letters are to have vertical and horizontal center lines and subsections measuring 4×4, knitting charts 15, 23, or 31 stitches wide are suitable, for instance. Also consider the sizes in relation to the thickness of the wool you're using and don't knit too loosely.

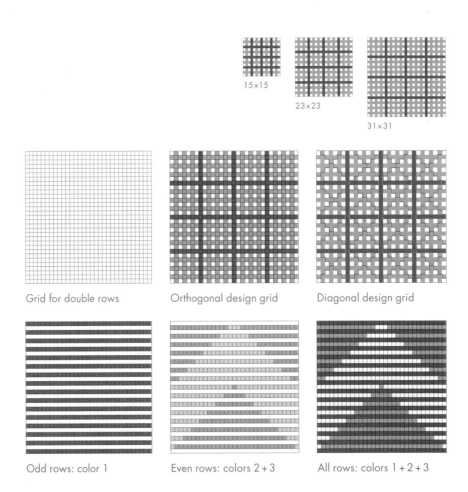

15×15

23×23

31×31

Grid for double rows

Orthogonal design grid

Diagonal design grid

Odd rows: color 1

Even rows: colors 2 + 3

All rows: colors 1 + 2 + 3

DIAGONAL STRIPE ^{KNIT}

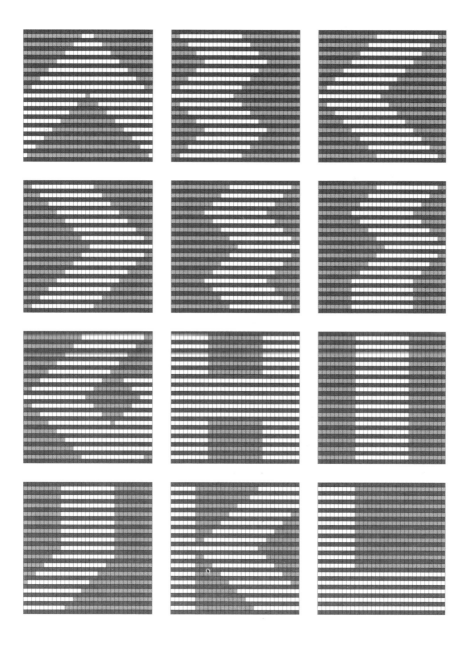

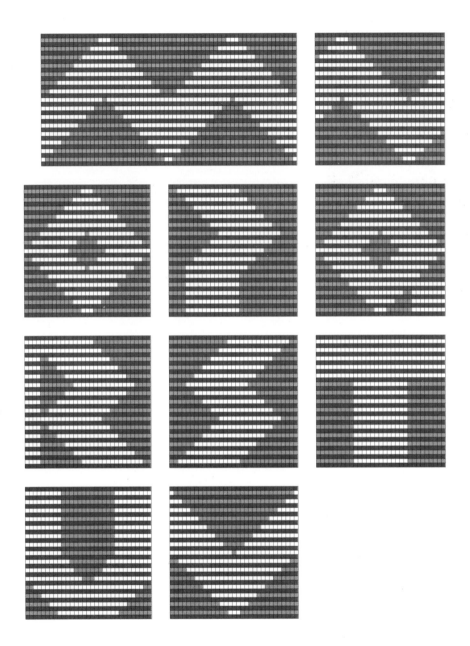

STRUCTURAL EFFECTS

To make the letter visible as a relief, knit the letters in stockinette stitch and garter stitch in color 2 only, with the change in stitch along the edge of the letter. On the double rows in color 1 make inverse changes from stockinette to garter stitch to those in color 2. When looking at the flat piece of knitting, you can only see a striped pattern. When viewed from an angle, however, the letter appears. This principle is illustrated in greater detail in *illusion* or *shadow knitting*. [→ p. 174]

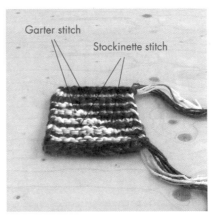

LIGHT EFFECTS

If you knit alternate patches together turned through 90 degrees—when making a blanket, for example—the entire surface takes on an additional optical effect as the light falls on the object.

When knitting letters with a design grid containing 45-degree diagonals, you also achieve extra visual effects when you turn the patches. The individual pieces are picked up and knitted from the edges or joined when finished.

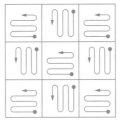

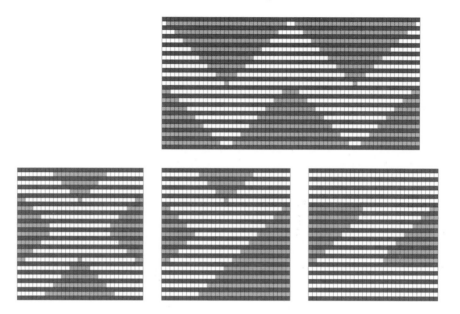

TEXTURAL VARIATIONS

With a few amendments, you can obtain a completely different result using the same type template.

You can turn the knitting direction 90 degrees and use garter stitch throughout. Instead of forming the letter only in even double rows, it can also be formed by a change in color from 1 and 3 on the odd rows and from colors 2 to 3 on the even rows [1].

Using a patterned yarn will make the letter appear blurred. Placing a joining stitch between the two pieces creates an additional visual accent [2].

FONT: DIAGONAL STRIPE ᴷᴺᴵᵀ [→ P. 107]
TECHNIQUE: DIAGONAL STRIPE [→ P. 104]

SLIP STITCHES AS LINES

For the basic pattern, knit alternate double rows in colors 1 and 2. Odd double rows are knitted in stockinette stitch throughout in color 1. Even double rows are knitted in color 2 and garter stitch. The letters are formed by slipping stitches in the odd rows in color 1.

To make slip stitches you slide the relevant stitches onto the right-hand needle without knitting them. Repeat this on the wrong-side rows, passing the unknitted yarn in front of your work (otherwise it later shows in front of the slipped stitch) [→ p. 86].

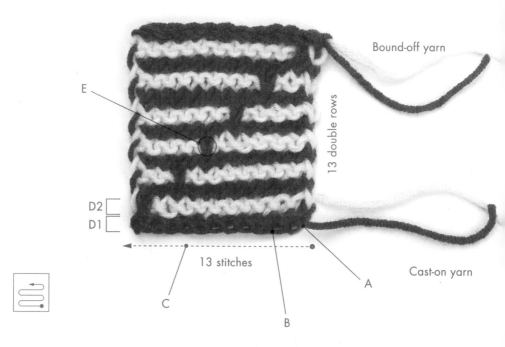

A	Cast-on loop
B	Cast-on row
C	Knitting direction
D1	Edge stitch for double row 1 (stockinette stitch)
D2	Edge stitch for double row 2 (garter stitch)
E	Slip stitch in color 1

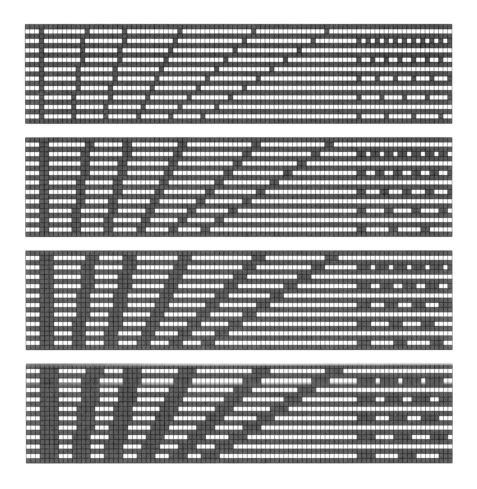

21

21

LINE THICKNESS AND ANGLE

To vary the line thickness, make several slip stitches one after the other. Note that this can pucker your knitting, so don't knit too tight. If you don't want to have too strong a horizontal running through the intermediate lines, you can knit horizontal lines as dotted lines.

STAGGERED SLIP STITCHES

If you make slip stitches in both the odd and even double rows, you create a shadow effect. In principle, this is also possible using three or more colors. So that you don't lose your place, you can allocate color groups to the odd or even, or stockinette or garter stitch double rows, for example.

SLIP-STITCH BACKS

This knitting technique is an easy way of creating visually interesting backs. If you knit your motifs as a mirror image, you can also use these as the front.

FONT: FUTUR X [→P. 202]
TECHNIQUE: SLIP STITCHES AS LINES [→P. 112]

SLIP STITCHES AS A GRID

Knit all odd double rows in color 1 and garter stitch for the basic slip-stitch pattern. Knit the even double rows in color 2 and garter stitch, lifting all odd stitches onto your right-hand needle without knitting them (these are the slip stitches that form the vertical grid). At the end of a right-side row you have alternate stitches in colors 1 and 2 on your needle.

Reverse this on the wrong-side rows: all the odd stitches (dark/color 1) are lifted onto your right-hand needle without being knitted. All even stitches (light/color 2) are knitted in the same color. When slipping the odd stitches, keep your yarn in front of your work; otherwise, it will later show on the right-side of your knitting. Once you've memorized this pattern, you can add color 3 in the even double rows (knitted with slip stitches in the same way as color 2) to make a letter.

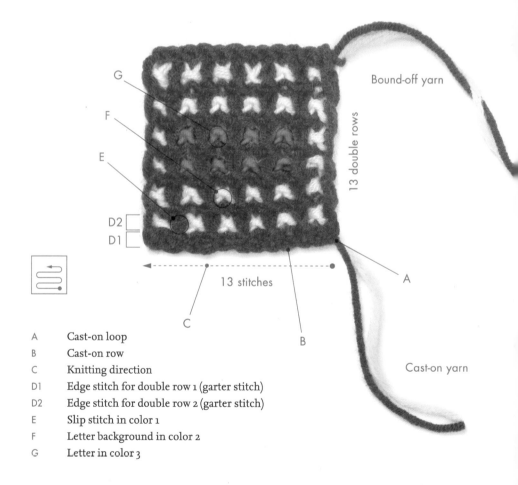

A	Cast-on loop
B	Cast-on row
C	Knitting direction
D1	Edge stitch for double row 1 (garter stitch)
D2	Edge stitch for double row 2 (garter stitch)
E	Slip stitch in color 1
F	Letter background in color 2
G	Letter in color 3

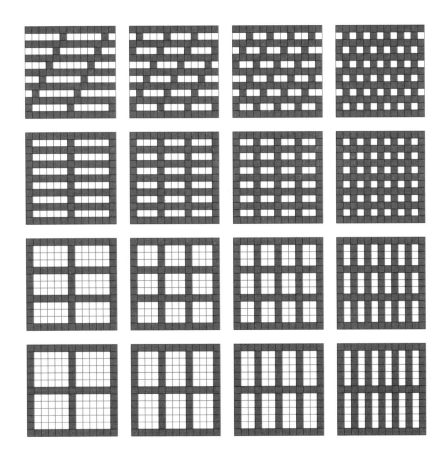

13

13

PATTERN VARIANTS

By changing the rhythm of the double rows and the slip stitches, you can fabricate countless variations of the basic pattern. Once your knitting techniques have suitably advanced, you can also stagger the slip stitches to make italic dot matrix fonts.

FONTS AND STRANDED YARNS

Basic slip-stitch patterns are relatively time-consuming to knit and better suited to more advanced knitters. Because the slip-stitch grid is knitted in color 1 and the letter in the background in colors 2 and 3 at the same time, things soon become rather confusing. You should take care to ensure that colors 1 and 2 are identical so that the structure is also the same in sections without a letter.

Depending on which font you're using and whether you want to knit a single letter [1], block of text [2], or repeat pattern [3], you end up with different lengths of stranded yarn. For clothing, it's best to use a typeface where the letter and background have a similar weight.

You can use dot matrix fonts as letters; with a good layout template you can also place any other typeface in a grid and scale and modify it until it fits the pattern [→ p.184].

Back of p.119

Back of p.43

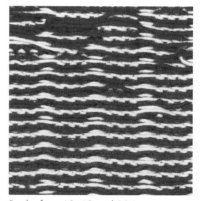

Back of pp.68–69 and 184

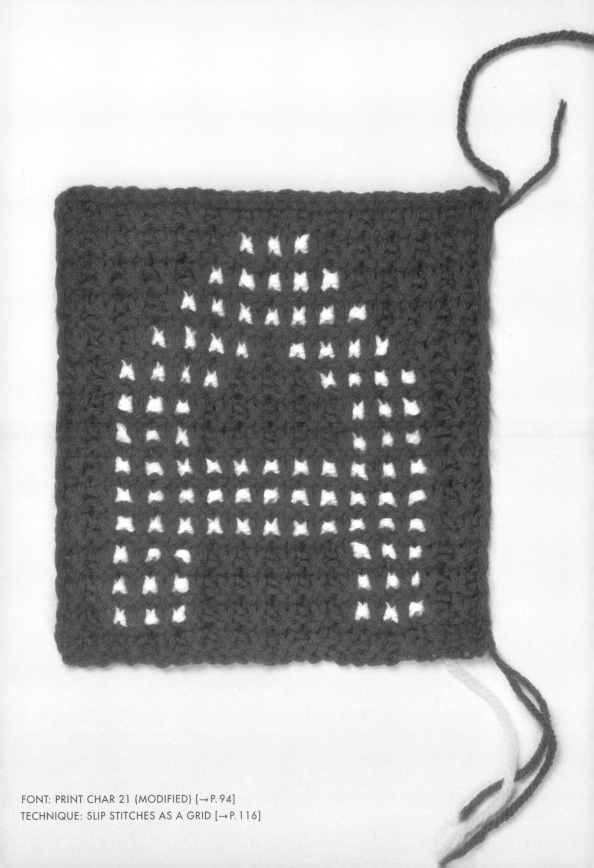

FONT: PRINT CHAR 21 (MODIFIED) [→ P. 94]
TECHNIQUE: SLIP STITCHES AS A GRID [→ P. 116]

TYPEJOCKEY ^{KNIT}

TypeJockey is an alphabet system by Andrea Tinnes consisting of 14 freely combinable fonts with different patterns. By layering the various weights, letters of intense color and complexity can be created. By contrast, the grid for the letter body is relatively simple. It comprises 36×36 pixels (40×40 including the edges), which are divided into 6×9 segments of 6×4 pixels each.

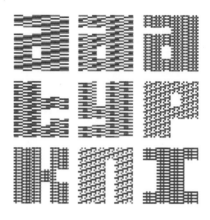

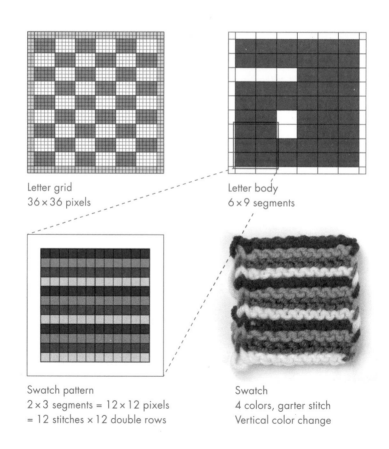

Letter grid
36 × 36 pixels

Letter body
6 × 9 segments

Swatch pattern
2 × 3 segments = 12 × 12 pixels
= 12 stitches × 12 double rows

Swatch
4 colors, garter stitch
Vertical color change

12 double rows
in garter stitch

3 double rows
in garter stitch
9 double rows in
stockinette stitch

12 double rows
in stockinette stitch

COMBINING STRUCTURE AND TEXTURE

In adapted TypeJockey [KNIT], the bodies of the letters have been adjusted to fit a grid of 6×9 or 12×18. The letter bodies and spaces have separate pattern repeats. Here, you can combine the knitting structure and color as you wish, thus varying the character of the letters.

As in the original, the letter bodies simply form a boundary from one repeat pattern to the next. Incidentally, you can also apply this principle to any other pixel font.

To find the perfect pattern for your letters, it's best to knit swatches of 2×3 segments or 12×12 pixels. One row of pixels equals 1 double row, giving you 12 stitches and 12 double rows.

When deciding on your structure, note that the height of knitting worked in garter stitch [1] contracts more strongly than when you alternate between garter and stockinette stitch [2]. Double rows in stockinette stitch [3] are about 1.5 times as high as double rows in garter stitch.

TESTING PATTERN COMBINATIONS

To start with, knit patterns that combine changes of color and structure. You can then increase the complexity. Start with a consistent structure, such as colors 1 and 2 in garter stitch [1]. Then introduce a change of structure and knit color 1 in garter stitch and color 2 in stockinette stitch [2]. Finally, add a third color with slip stitches, first using two colors per row [3] and then changing color in the row, giving you three colors per row [4].

The more you make your color patterns and knitting structures independent of one another, the more playful your result [5]. It's also worth applying some digital design to the project at this point: knit up multicolored patterns in basic colors, such as red, green, yellow, and blue. In a Photoshop mock-up, you can then play with the individual colors and try out various contrasts and shades of color. Then go back to your analog knitting.

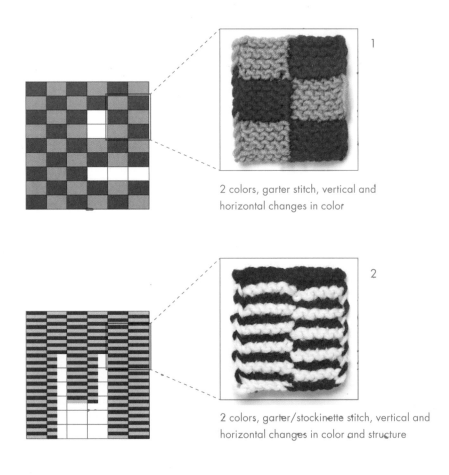

1

2 colors, garter stitch, vertical and horizontal changes in color

2

2 colors, garter/stockinette stitch, vertical and horizontal changes in color and structure

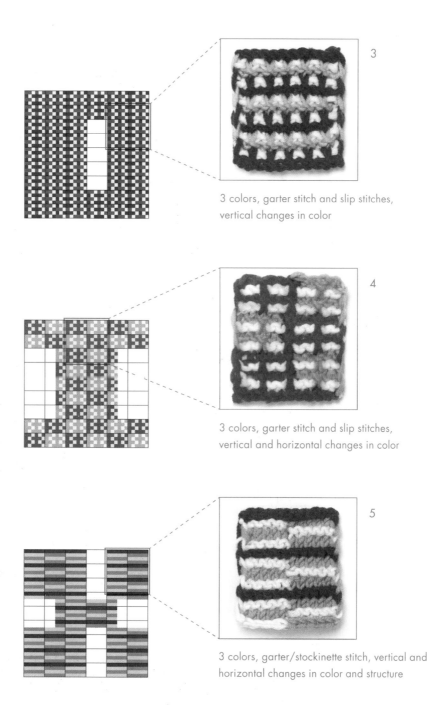

3

3 colors, garter stitch and slip stitches, vertical changes in color

4

3 colors, garter stitch and slip stitches, vertical and horizontal changes in color

5

3 colors, garter/stockinette stitch, vertical and horizontal changes in color and structure

TYPEJOCKEY ^{KNIT}   DESIGN: ANDREA TINNES   TYPECUTS

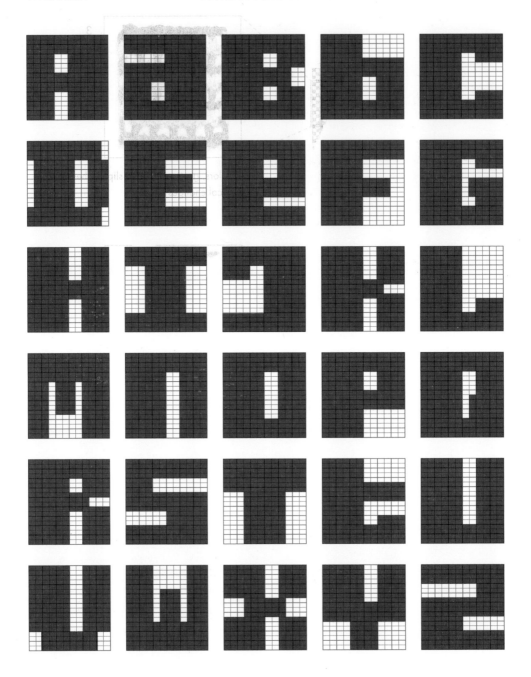

FONT: TYPEJOCKEY^{KNIT} [→PP. 120–125]
TECHNIQUE: FAIR ISLE [→P. 92]

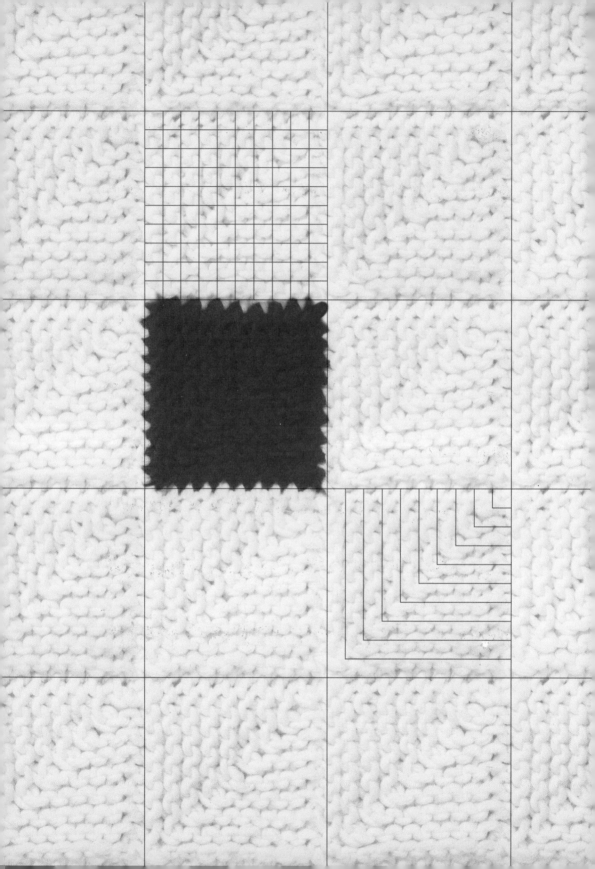

IV

PATCHES

Large-format pixel fonts
with simple patchwork knitting

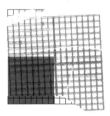

Patch-based knitting is suitable for large-format single letters and short words on sweaters, cushions, or blankets. Simple pixel fonts or enlarged screenshots act as a template; images rendered in large pixels are also possible.

CORNER PATCH

Corner patches—or what are more commonly known as *mitred squares*—constitute the basic element in patch-based knitting. Knit at least 11×11 stitches to produce a patch measuring approximately 2×2 in. (5×5 cm), depending on the yarn used. With a letter pattern comprising 3×5 units, single letters of approximately 6×10 in. (15×25 cm) are produced.

These sizes can be enlarged at will; for smaller units, stitch-based knitting is recommended [→ p.89].

The alignment of the single patch is important when knitting on the next patches. The cast-on row, which counts as the right-side row of the first double row, is knitted from right to left. The cast-on strand of yarn is therefore always on the bottom right, with the bind off on the top right.

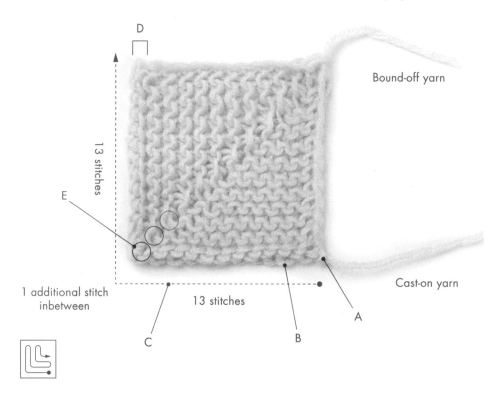

D

Bound-off yarn

13 stitches

E

1 additional stitch inbetween

13 stitches

C

B

A

Cast-on yarn

A	Cast-on loop
B	Cast-on row
C	Knitting direction
D	Edge stitch for a double row
E	Knit three stitches together on a wrong-side row

KNITTING A CORNER PATCH

Always think in double rows when knitting a patch. The right- and wrong-side rows form a unit and are in the same color. A corner patch takes on its square shape from the garter stitch double rows and the corner. The corner is made by always knitting the three center stitches together on the wrong-side row. You can also see this in the two diagrams, with [1] showing the rows and [2] the target shape.

Once you've memorized this principle, you only need to count the stitches on the cast-on row. You then continue knitting stitches together or reducing the number of stitches on the wrong-side rows until just one stitch is left. Thread the yarn through the last stitch and slowly pull it tight.

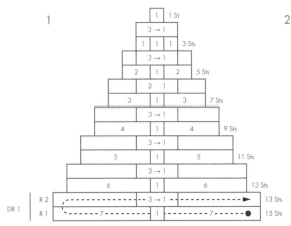

Diagram as rows (Patch size 7×7 stitches)

Diagram as target shape

St(s)	Stitch(es)
R	Row
DR	Double row
3 → 1	Knit three stitches together

KNITTING ON PATCHES

The knitting direction of a simple corner patch runs diagonally from bottom left to top right. Neighboring patches are knit onto the first patch in the same direction. You either add the next patch to the right or along the top of the first one. You cast on stitches to make the bottom or left edges of the new patches.

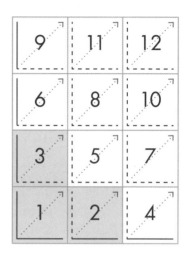

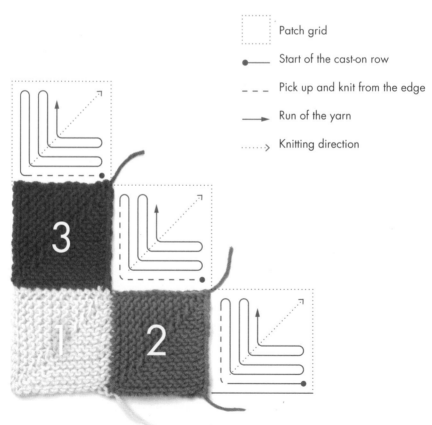

Patch grid

Start of the cast-on row

Pick up and knit from the edge

Run of the yarn

Knitting direction

FURTHER PREPARATIONS

The size of an individual patch depends on many factors: yarn thickness, needle size, stitch count, patch structure (garter stitch is more compact than alternate garter and stockinette stitch) and—last but not least—your individual style of knitting. This is why you should always knit a few swatches before starting on the full letter.

Once you've determined the patch size, you can simplify the knitting process further by undoing, or "ripping," a patch, measuring the length of yarn, and cutting pieces of yarn of the same length. This means that you avoid annoying knots in your yarn, especially when doing colorwork.

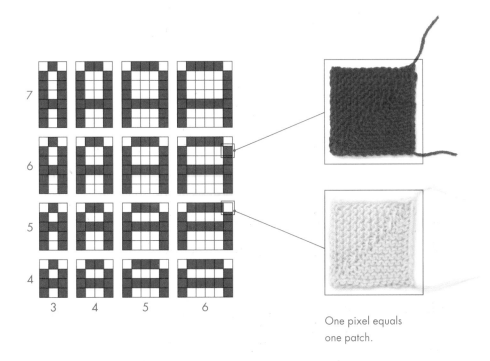

One pixel equals one patch.

When selecting the pixel font you want to use, the finished size of your knitting may be determinative—or the font is allowed to influence the final format of your work. You can always also modify individual letters for additional fine adjustment.

KK FIXED 4 × 5   KREATIVE KORPORATION

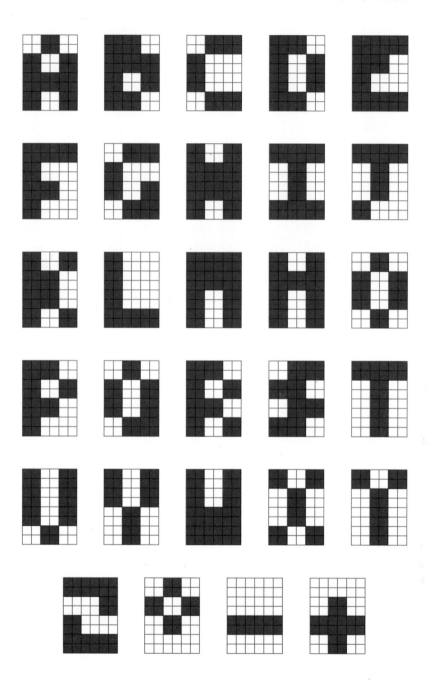

FONT: KK FIXED 4×5 [→P.132]
TECHNIQUE: CORNER PATCH [→P.128]

CORNER PATCH WITH COLOR CHANGES

The easiest way of lending corner patches greater graphic individuality is to change color within the patch. To do so, simply leave the yarn in color 1 hanging at the end of a wrong-side row and continue the next right-side row in color 2. You can weave in the loose end of color 1 into the back of your work with the next neighboring patch.

You can vary color changes within a patch completely at random. To check whether your pattern variant matches the letter design, you could make a rough collage—in Excel or Photoshop, or manually using copied test patches. The Vectoraster program [→ p. 212] is also good for creating more complex raster patterns with a font or pictorial motif.

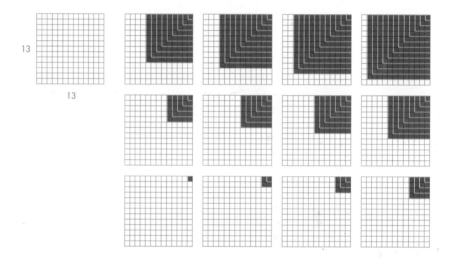

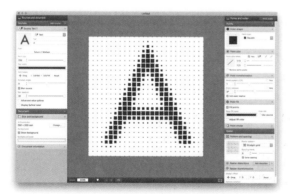

You can simulate images and fonts in the Vectoraster program.

FONT: MONTEREY [→P.189]
TECHNIQUE: CORNER PATCH
WITH COLOR CHANGES

COLOR GRADING

If you want to knit an enlarged anti-aliased image of a font, you need various shades of a single yarn. However, not all types of yarn are available in a range of different hues.

If this is the case, you can sort the available yarns by brightness and allocate these to the various colors on the template. If you grade the different shades by their brightness, you achieve an effect similar to the Photoshop hue/saturation filter.

You can also grade colors directly when knitting by combining single yarns: two shades of yarn produce four grades of color, for example. In this way, with slightly bigger needles you can easily mix four to five yarns to produce as many intermediate shades.

Mixing yarns is also a good way of using up your scraps. The result is all the more voluminous. To compensate for this, you can use thinner yarns or bigger needles.

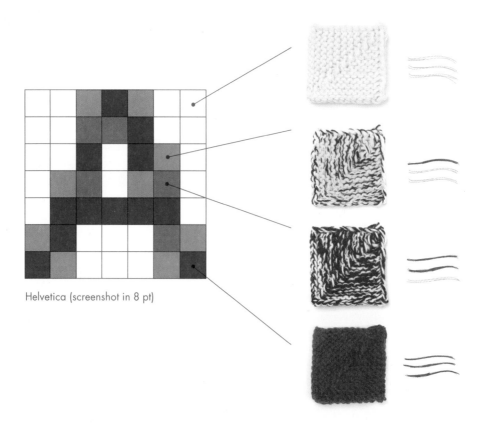

Helvetica (screenshot in 8 pt)

V.

MODULES

Large-format modular fonts
with advanced patchwork knitting

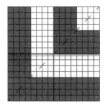

In patch-based knitting with modules the patches are worked in more than one color, generating bold patterns and structures. This permits a wide variety of letter variations, which take on a strong graphic character thanks to their stripes, right angles, and forty-five degree diagonals. Module knitting is especially suitable for large objects, such as cushions or blankets, where the graphic character is given particular emphasis.

CORNER PATCH MODULES

Taking the single-color corner patch as a basis [→ p. 128], the corner patch module is embellished with changes of color and structure. You knit a double row in one color. Odd double rows are knitted in garter stitch, even double rows in stockinette stitch. This produces a relief structure that lends the result a tactile quality and a certain shadow play.

When changing color the first yarn is put aside at the end of the first double row and the next double row knitted in the second color. This basic pattern can be adapted very easily. You can also use a third or fourth color to additionally accentuate letter stems within several double rows.

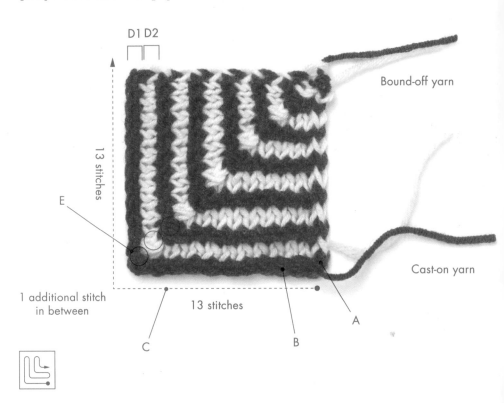

A   Cast-on loop
B   Cast-on row
C   Knitting direction
D1   Edge stitch for double row 1 (garter stitch)
D2   Edge stitch for double row 2 (stockinette stitch)
E   Knit three stitches together on a **wrong-side row**
F   Color change

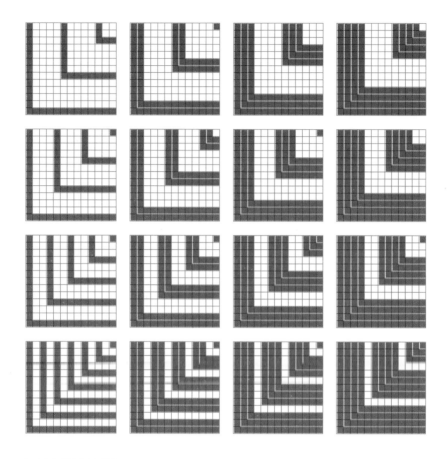

13

13

PATTERN VARIANTS

Various numbers of stitches are suitable for corner patch modules depending on the pattern used. The following shows several variants of a 13×13-stitch patch. To gain a feel for the size and pattern characteristics, it's useful to first knit up a few big patches, take photos of them, and then make digital collages of a bunch of different letters.

BASIC CORNER PATCH MODULES

By doubling, tripling, or quadrupling the number of cast-on stitches, you can extend the corner patch module to make a half, three-quarter, or full square. You continue to knit the three center stitches of each quarter segment together on a wrong-side row.

When making a full square you then close the remaining gap by knitting the sides together as when joining pieces of knitting [→ p.87]. Or simply sew up the two sides using a seam stitch.

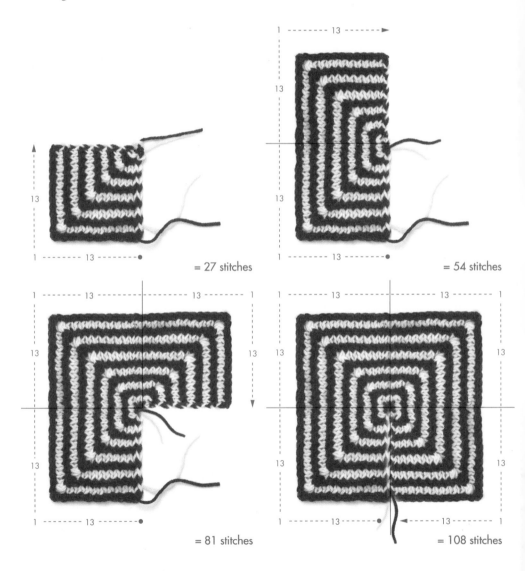

= 27 stitches

= 54 stitches

= 81 stitches

= 108 stitches

SEGMENTS MADE FROM BASIC MODULES

The ends of the basic corner patch modules can be extended in the direction of your knitting as you require. This helps them to form characteristic knitting segments to make letters. Keep these segments as simple as possible to make it easier to knit the pieces together at a later stage.

To start with, don't mix up the alignment of the corners in order to keep things simple. You have to increase the number of stitches in the center at one corner [1] instead of knitting the three center stitches together as usual [2].

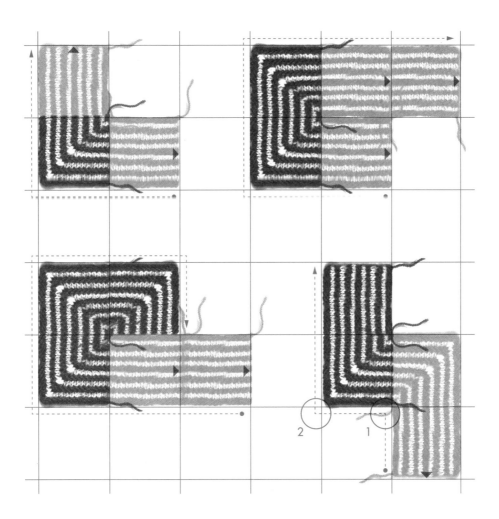

CONSTRUCTING LETTERS

You can construct letters in two different ways: if you're aiming for an exact final format, you end up with a patch grid that you have to work from. The second method is to develop the letter first and then fill up the final format with patches. This is easier and makes more sense when you're just starting to knit modules. When designing the letters, also try to envision the final format in single patches or in individual knitting segments.

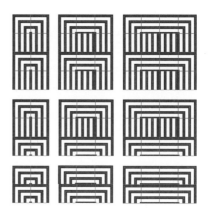

Patch grid variants

Individual patch   Knitting segment   Final format

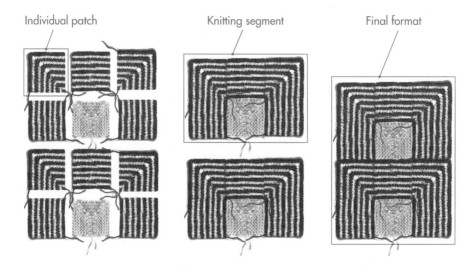

You can't always render all letters with a single patch type and within one grid. For example, the counter in this letter A needs a workaround: this involves simply continuing to knit the corner patches together to the center.

KNITTING ON SEGMENTS

You knit one segment of a letter onto the
next one in a certain consecutive order.
Each segment is knitted to the previous
segment along its respective cast-on edge
[→ p. 84]. Before you start knitting, plan
the best order in which to make and link
up the different segments.

You can join most segment combinations
in this manner. If necessary, adjust the
letters slightly. Only in rare cases do you
have to knit any remaining sections
together once you've knitted everything
else [→ p. 87].

Patch grid

Start of the cast-on row

Pick up and knit from the edge

Run of the yarn

Knitting direction

Bind off

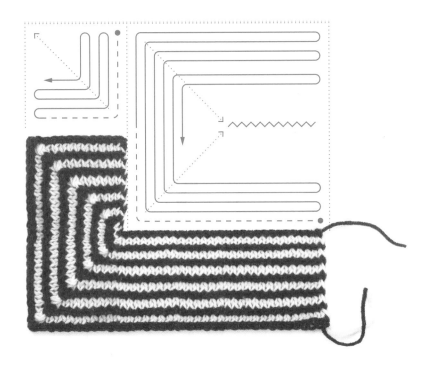

All variants of this *A* can be knitted in two segments.

This colored counter can be created by changing color within the patch.

This *B* can be knitted in one piece from the outside to the inside. The innermost line is bound off.

Segment 1
Segment 2

Cast-on row

This *C* is bound off along the inner line. It can appear thicker when knitted than on the layout.

This *C* can be knitted in one piece and is similar to segment 1 in the *A*.

To knit these corners, the white inside section must be knitted on as a separate segment.

PROTOTYPING

When designing a font, switch between analog and digital prototyping. Knit up some individual patches [1], photograph them, and make uniform mock-up modules [2]. You can then immerse yourself with these in the digital design phase in any layout program [3].

Subsequently, first knit a few of the letters that could contain difficult details. The letter R probably has more details than an L, for instance. Once you have gained some practical experience from this example, you can then continue to work on your digital design in Photoshop [4]. Repeat this or a similar procedure as often as you need to.

To gain a feel for possible forms of design and to better anticipate the knitted result, to start with it's worth frequently changing between analog and digital forms of prototyping.

1

Sample patch

2

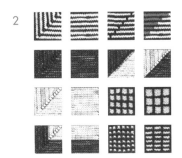

Mock-up modules

4

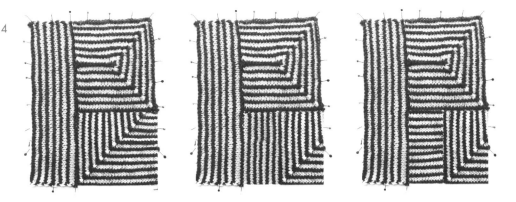

Variants in Photoshop

SINGLE LETTERS VS. FONTS

There's a big difference between making single letters and creating entire fonts. Some methods of construction work better for one letter than for others. You can gain some experience here by prototyping individual letters.

If you wish to attempt an entire alphabet, it's best to also create a knitting diagram where you note down the order in which the various modules and segments are knitted. In this way, you can simply pass on your font for testing—on Ravelry, for instance—and at the same time obtain feedback on the comprehensibility of your templates and patterns.

MODUL CORNER KNIT

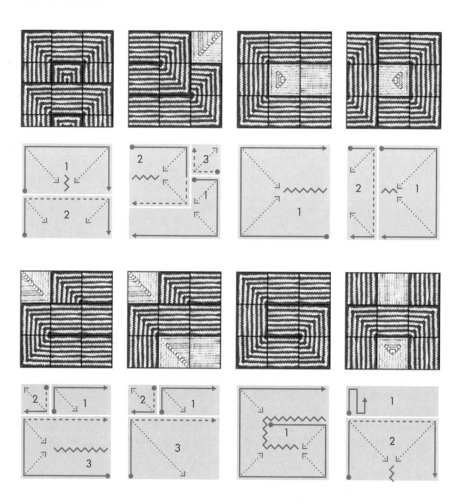

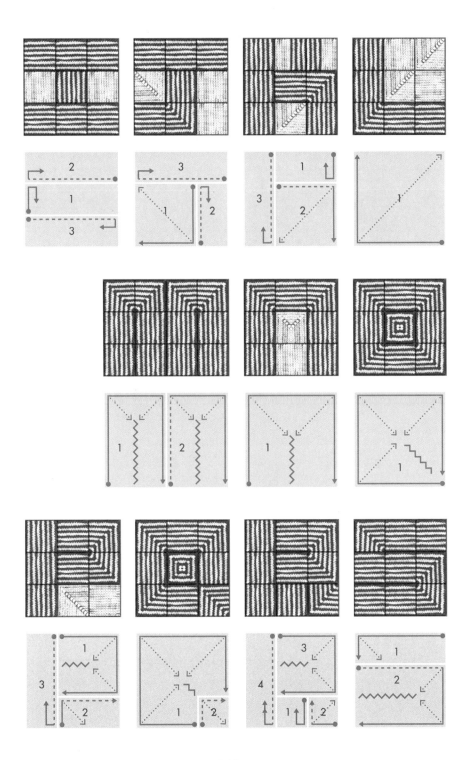

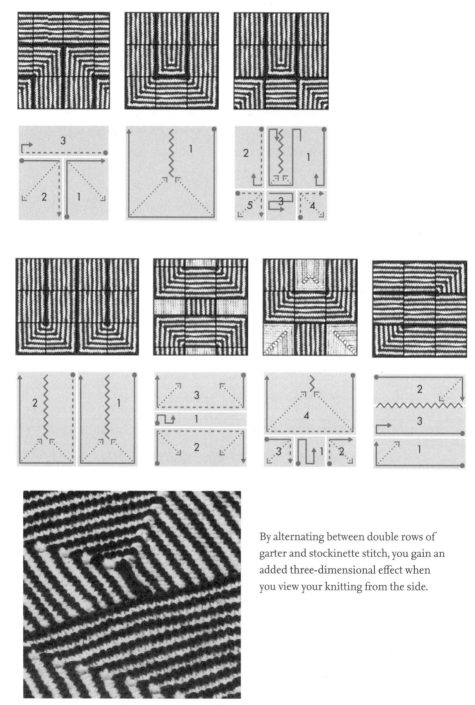

By alternating between double rows of garter and stockinette stitch, you gain an added three-dimensional effect when you view your knitting from the side.

FONT: MODUL CORNER KNIT [→ P. 148]
TECHNIQUE: CORNER PATCH
MODULE [→ P. 140]

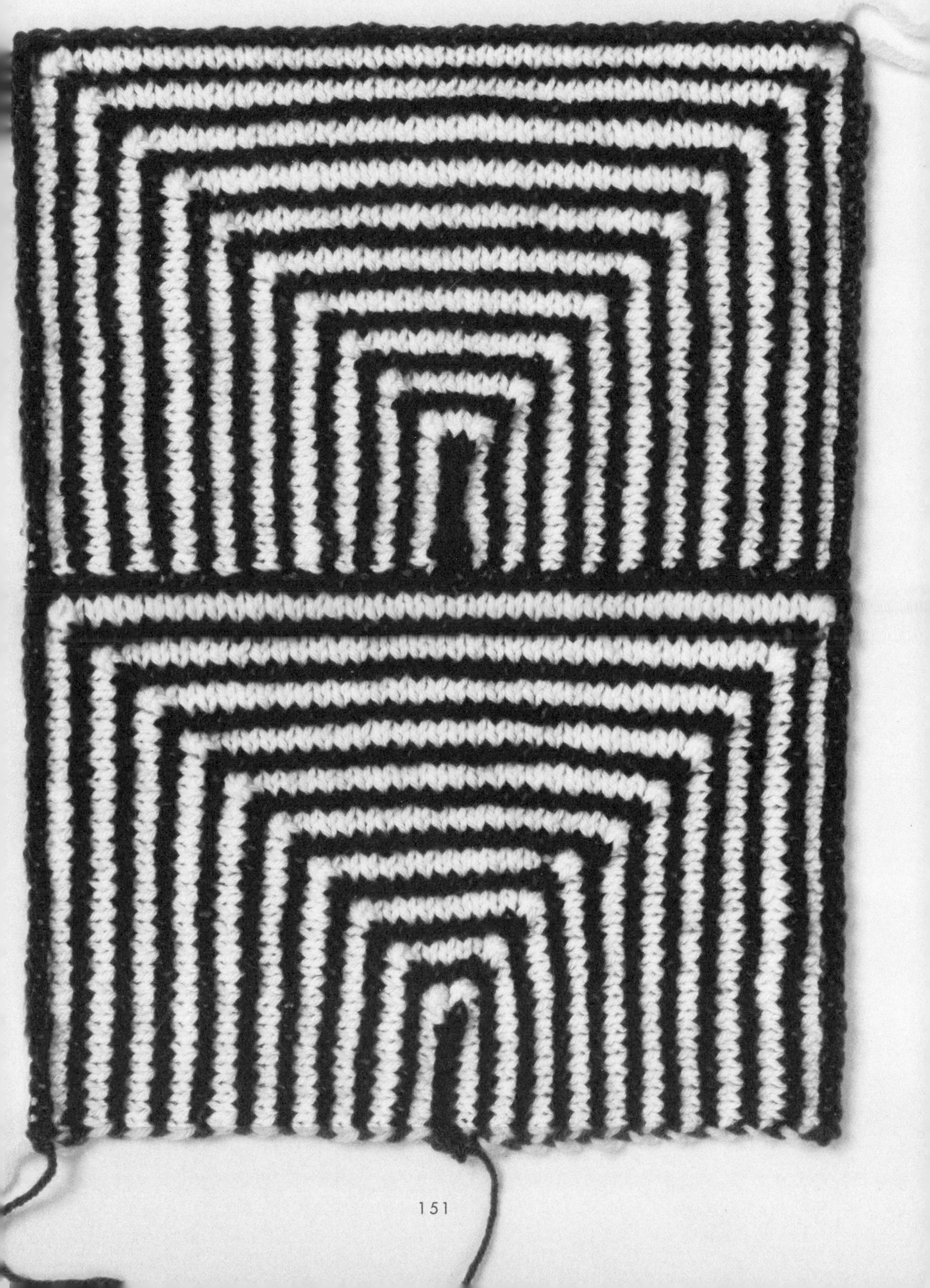

DIAGONAL CORNER PATCHES

A diagonal corner patch is constructed in the same way as a corner patch, with the difference being that the color changes in the middle of each right- and wrong-side row. These diagonals make a striking visual element. The extra stitch in the middle is not needed here: on a wrong-side row two stitches in colors 1 and 2, respectively, are knitted together before and after the color change. Two stitches are thus decreased on each wrong-side row. Between them the yarns are twisted together. As you change color on every right- and wrong-side row, this patch takes slightly longer to knit but has an interesting basic pattern.

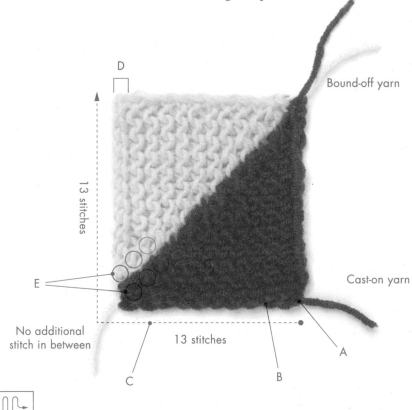

A   Cast-on loop
B   Cast-on row
C   Knitting direction
D   Edge stitch for a double row
E   Knit two stitches together per color on the wrong-side row and twist the yarns

VARIANTS AND SEGMENTS

The diagonal corner patch can also be knitted up into half, three-quarter, or full squares, and expanded like the corner patch module [→ p. 143]. Here, you can also incorporate 90-degree color changes. Making segments with this method requires a little more getting used to than with corner patches, as the dominant diagonals are contrary to the knitting direction. The diagonals can be put to good use as bold serifs.

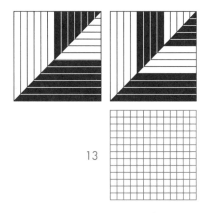

13

13

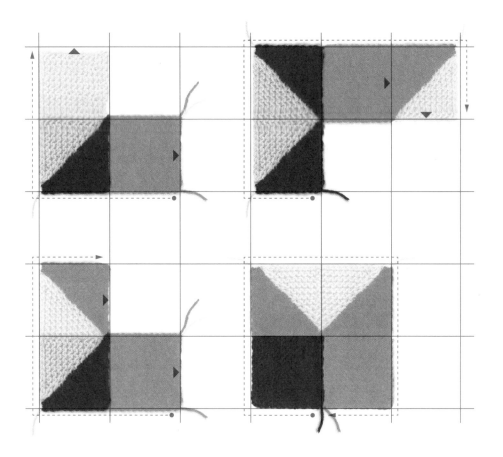

PHOENIX KNIT CHRISTIAN SCHMALOHR

Phoenix merges a black-letter typeface with a technological language of form. Basing it on a broken typeface means that the line thicknesses have a high contrast. In Phoenix KNIT, the majuscules are knitted based on diagonal corner patches to lend the serifs particular emphasis. The different line thicknesses are created by changing yarn within a corner patch segment and can be flexibly adapted.

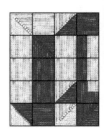

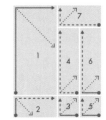

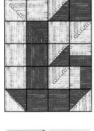
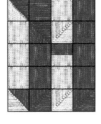
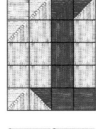
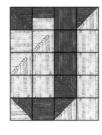
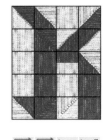

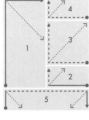
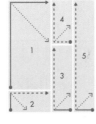
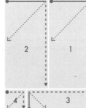
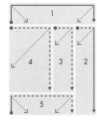
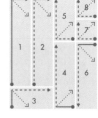

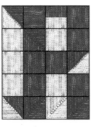
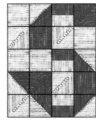
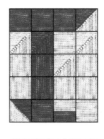
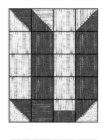

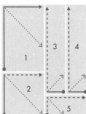
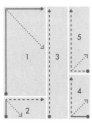
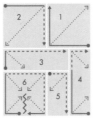

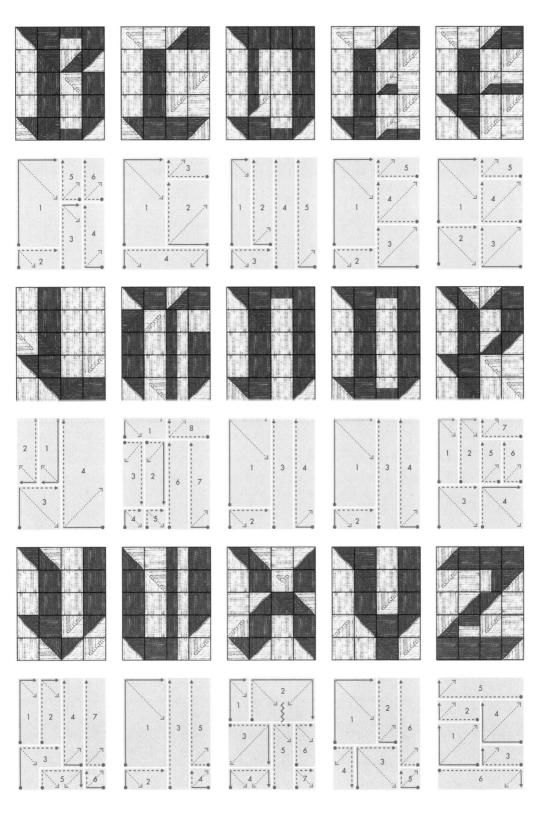

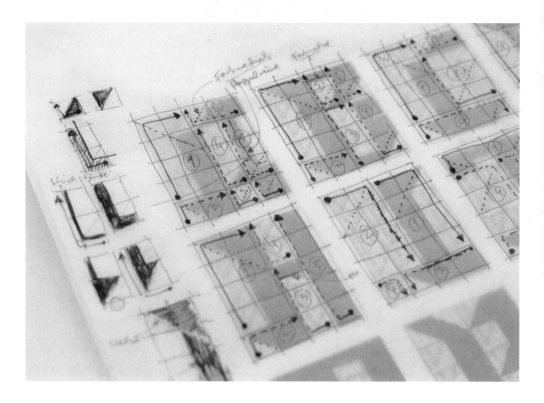

FORMING SEGMENTS

As with corner patch modules, segments are also formed here to simplify the knitting process [→ p. 144]. With diagonal corner patches, it's slightly more difficult to find the perfect order for the various knitting segments. The reason is that the sloped lines don't indicate the knitting direction but show the diagonals formed when the center stitches are knitted together. This initially makes the individual segments less distinct.

Don't be confused by this, however! Lay some tracing paper on your design and clearly sketch in the differences between the cast-on rows (dot with an unbroken line) and the rows that have been picked up and knitted (dotted line). Also draw in the central diagonals. This gradually gives you an overview and provides you with a kind of design grid for the other letters.

If, as in the above example, you wish to use a second letter color, you can also place color changes that do not lie on the diagonal. First, plan a couple of sample letters, and then apply this basic principle to the remaining letters in your font.

FONT: PHOENIX KNIT [→ P. 154]
TECHNIQUE: DIAGONAL CORNER
PATCH [→ P. 152]

COMBINING PATTERNS AND MODULES

As soon as you've explored the various characteristics of the pattern and module types, you can combine these at will. By the way, in patchwork knitting you can also knit patches onto the sides of other patches. This is explained in more detail in books that deal with this technique [→ p. 213].

The procedure that combines different types of patches is basically the same: define a patch grid and a uniform number of stitches per single patch. While designing, also think about the order in which your segments can be joined.

During the design process, continue to switch between analog and digital prototyping. As soon as you've sufficiently explored the characteristics of the various patch types, you can do much of your work in the layout program or make use of font editors, such as Glyphs or FontLab [→ p. 212].

One free alternative for simple designs is the FontStruct font-building tool—you can design alphabets online and then download them as a font. The individual modules can be combined to make *composite bricks* that match your patch types.

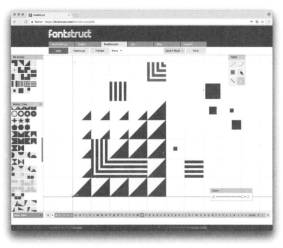

In the FontStruct font editor, you can select existing modules or combine new ones.

FONT: CUSTOM (FONTSTRUCT)
TECHNIQUE: MODULE,
DIAGONAL CORNER PATCH [→P. 152]

VI.

PROJECT TEMPLATES

Select knitting patterns

After working on your first test patches and experimental letters, you can now apply your *typeknitting* skills to the fabrication of entire objects. This section contains several sample patterns showing how to modify existing knitting patterns or make your own designs. You can find many more patterns on Ravelry, for example. Before you start a project, it's always a good idea to knit a few swatches or test patches first to gain an idea of the texture and sizing.

MOVABLE TYPE CUSHION

Turn your couch into a hall of fame showcasing your *typeknitting* skills, and a creative playground for movable type! With cushions, you can experiment with type and patterns without having to think about the cut and wearability of the finished object. Square or rectangular shapes are suitable for all techniques and sizes. You can also join all of the test letters and patches you've fashioned to date to make a sampler.

You don't really need a knitting pattern for cushion covers. The back and front have the same format and are knitted together at the sides [→ p. 87]. Include an edge of about .5–.75 in. (1–2 cm) as this will disappear inside the cushion when you knit it up. On the back, you should also add a flap with buttonholes.

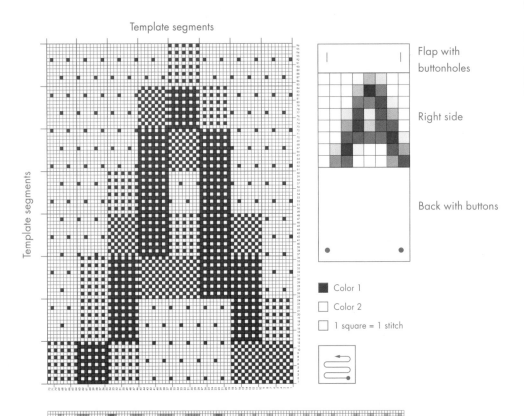

Template segments

Template segments

Flap with buttonholes

Right side

Back with buttons

■ Color 1

☐ Color 2

☐ 1 square = 1 stitch

ABCDEFGHIJKLMN
OPQRSTUVWXYZ#

Helvetica (screenshot in 10 pt)

FONT: HELVETICA 8 PT (MAX MIEDINGER)
TECHNIQUE: GRAYSCALING WITH KNITTING PATTERNS [→ P. 100]
MATERIALS: LANA GROSSA BINGO (5-MM/US 8/UK 6 NEEDLES)

REMIX FAN SCARF

No digital fan club is complete without a remix fan scarf! Collect pixel diagrams of team scarves and knit your own message or hashtag.

To make the template, create a file in Photoshop with a pixel ratio that matches the stitch height of the scarf. A good average is 40–46 stitches or pixels. Then export the graphic as a PNG file with the required number of colors. (Incidentally, the poorer and noisier the graphic template, the more interesting the *dithering* effect.)

A pixel diagram or photographed collage can also be converted into a knitting pattern using KnitPro [→ p. 212].

Modify the template [→ p. 25] and knit using the Fair Isle or intarsia technique. Use two- or three-color intarsia for the separate letter sections. The cast-on edge is the short side; choose the knitting direction depending on the motif [→ p. 22]. To stop the scarf from curling, alternately knit two and purl two stitches.

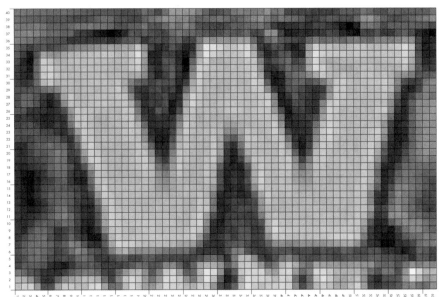

KnitPro automatically translates the pixel dimensions of your image template.

FONT: FAN SCARF ELEMENTS
PROCESS: COLOR REDUCTION, PIXEL REPEATS
TECHNIQUE: INTARSIA, STOCKINETTE AND GARTER STITCH [→ P.192]

DOUBLE-FACE HAT

With the double-face technique, you knit the front and back simultaneously so that you can wear your finished hat reversed. It also producer a thicker, more robust garment. As with double-face, it's easier to increase stitches than to decrease them, so knit the hat from the top down.

The basic hat element has a width of 10 stitches. These basic elements are repeated eight times to give you a total width of 80 stitches. Using 6-mm (US 10/UK 4) needles, the hat has a head circumference of 20.5 in. (52 cm). For larger sizes, use bigger needles or thicker yarn.

Your motif can be read best in rows 30 to 59. You can use a pattern repeat of 10 (eight repeats), 20 (four repeats), or 40 (two repeats) stitches or knit the design across the entire width of the hat.

If you want to knit a loop or infinity scarf instead of a hat, in rows 1–17 knit all 80 stitches, including the stitches otherwise omitted.

You can find some good examples and instructions on the internet using the search term "double knitting" [→ p. 213].

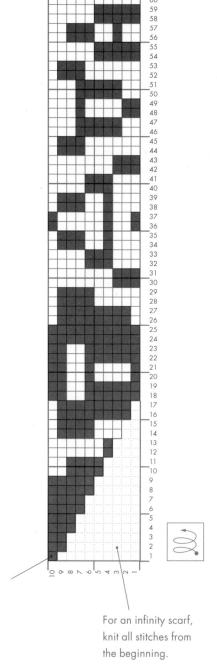

For the hat, only cast on every tenth stitch and increase in the following 16 rows.

For an infinity scarf, knit all stitches from the beginning.

FONT: ELEMENTAR [→ PP.193–195]
TECHNIQUE: DOUBLE-FACE [→ P.93], STOCKINETTE STITCH [→ P.78]
MATERIALS: LANG YARNS MERINO+ (6-MM/US 10/UK 4 NEEDLES)
PATTERN: MERET BÜTZBERGER

Color 1   Color 2

1 square = 1 stitch

SELBU MITTENS

These gloves are based on the classic Norwegian *Selbuvotter*, which 15-year-old shepherd Marit Gulsetbrua from Selbu in Norway devised in 1857.

You can find numerous interpretations on Ravelry, such as Adrian Bizilia's Generic Norwegian Mittens chart from Ravelry, on which this pattern is also based.

You can easily insert your own initials or patterns on the blank template. You can also knit in secret messages in Morse code and braille along the edges and on the rib.

The mittens are knitted with a set of double-pointed needles using the Fair Isle technique. If you don't have some experience in colorwork and knitting socks, you may find yourself constantly dropping the five needles!

If, in your motif, a yarn is stranded for seven stitches or more on the reverse, weave it in so that your fingers don't get caught up in it when you put your finished mittens on. Small pattern repeats are thus especially suitable here as the yarn is only stranded for a couple of stitches.

MORSE CODE

BRAILLE

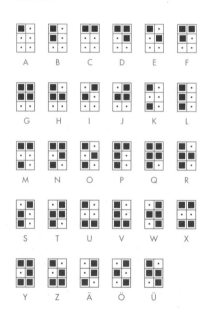

- ■ Dot = 1 Stitch
- ■■■ Dash = 3 Stitches
- □ Space between parts of the same letter
- □□ Space between two letters
- □□□ Space between two words

FONT: GEM DESKTOP 2.0 [→ P.192]
TECHNIQUE: FAIR ISLE [→ P.92], STOCKINETTE STITCH [→ P.78], KNIT IN THE ROUND
MATERIALS: LANG YARNS MERINO+ (4.5-MM/US/UK 7 NEEDLES)
PATTERN: ADRIAN BIZILIA

Morse code

Braille

INSTRUCTIONS

Swatch: it's very important to knit a swatch here, as Fair Isle knits up tighter than other knitting styles (the stitches have an aspect ratio of almost 1:1). Knitting 24–25 stitches across 4 inches (or 6 stitches per inch) in sport weight wool makes a mitten 8 inches in circumference and 12 inches long. This is a women's small or child's medium mitten.

Sizes: to make your mittens larger or smaller, use a different needle size and thinner or thicker yarn. Aim for a size that is about .75 in. (1.5 cm) larger than the circumference of your hand measured across the palm. For child's sizes, use a yarn that is suitable for 2–3-mm (US 0–2.5 / UK 14–11) needles, for men yarn for 4–4.5-mm (US 6–7 / UK 8–7) needles.

Pattern: loosely cast on 48 stitches in color 1. Knit one round in stockinette stitch. Join color 2 and knit a 1×1 rib, knitting color 1 and purling color 2. Continue according to the pattern when rib measures 1.5–2 in. (4–5 cm). Knit the motif on the top- and underside in color 2, and the Morse code along the sides in color 1.

Thumbs: knit in a scrap of wool along the thumb line, sliding the same stitches back onto the left-hand needle and knitting them again in the pattern. Once you've finished the mitten, remove the scrap of wool, place the stitches on your needles, and knit the thumb from this point onward.

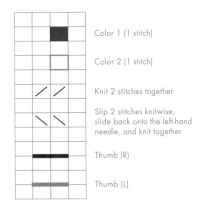

Color 1 (1 stitch)

Color 2 (1 stitch)

Knit 2 stitches together

Slip 2 stitches knitwise, slide back onto the left-hand needle, and knit together

Thumb (R)

Thumb (L)

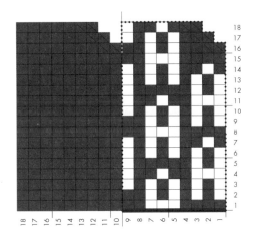

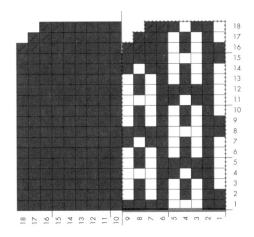

ILLUSION KNITTING BLANKET

The *illusion knitting* method (or *shadow knitting*) is based on alternate double rows in two colors. The motif is formed in color 1 by the change from garter to stockinette stitch (and vice versa in color 2). The relief structure this creates is only visible when viewed from an angle.

With a little preparation, you can also knit pictorial motifs using this technique. You can find a tutorial showing you how to make your own knitting patterns online [→p.213].

Start

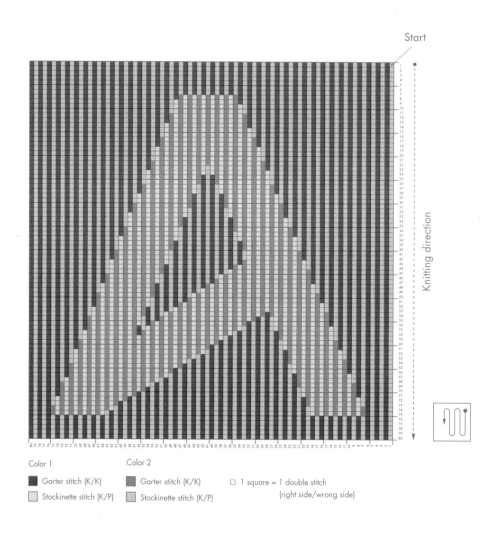

Knitting direction

Color 1

■ Garter stitch (K/K)

▨ Stockinette stitch (K/P)

Color 2

▨ Garter stitch (K/K)

▨ Stockinette stitch (K/P)

□ 1 square = 1 double stitch
(right side/wrong side)

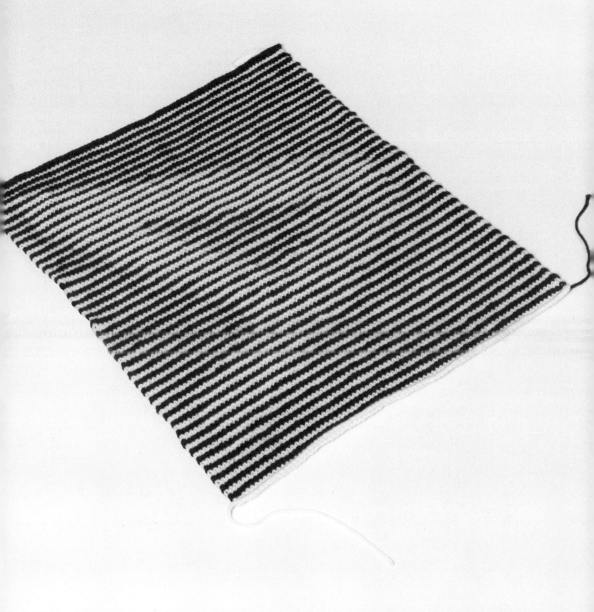

FONT: LŸNO (KARL NAWROT & RADIM PESKO) [→ P.212]
TECHNIQUE: ILLUSION KNITTING, STOCKINETTE AND GARTER STITCH [→ P.109]
MATERIALS: LANA GROSSA COOL WOOL BIG (4.5-MM/US/UK 7 NEEDLES)
PATTERN: PAT ASHFORTH AND STEVE PLUMMER

PATCHWORK SWEATER

This sweater is made with single-color patches knitted in garter stitch. You should have some experience in patchwork knitting for this project [→ p. 80]. Use a screenshot or Photoshop file in 72 ppi as your design, the pixel ratio of which equals the number of patches later used. Reduce the number of document colors to the required quantity and enlarge the motif using the *pixel repeat* option.

For your materials, select types of yarn with the necessary number of shades or mix several yarns together [→ p. 136]. When knitting, note that sweaters stretch easily as they are heavy by nature, so knit tight rather than too loosely.

For the pattern of the garment, take basic oblong shapes as your basis. The neck opening is at the apex of the letter. Calculate the exact measurements of the various sections from a sweater you can use as a reference. Make a paper pattern on which to draw the patch grid.

The nature of patchwork knitting helps you to adjust the garment shape as you can simply add or remove patches as you need them. First knit the front, back, and arms, and loosely crochet them together on the wrong side using a latch hook. This allows you to try the sweater on and modify it as you knit. Add ribbing to the sweater to finish it.

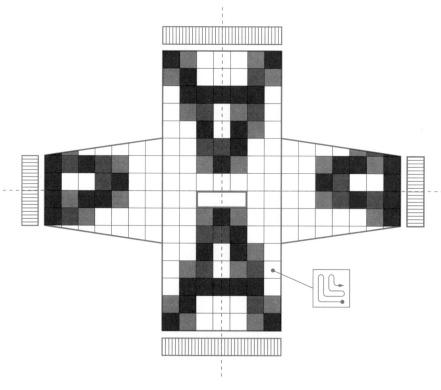

FONT: HELVETICA (MAX MIEDINGER)
TECHNIQUE: CORNER PATCH (11×11 STITCHES) [→ PP. 81, 128]
MATERIALS: LANG YARNS MERINO 50 (9-MM/US 13/UK 00 NEEDLES)

SLIP-STITCH SWEATER

To knit a sweater with a more elaborate font, either take a sweater that fits you well and make a paper pattern of it or modify an existing pattern.

You can find simple knitting patterns with a list of the materials you need on Ravelry, Pinterest, or a yarn manufacturer's website. Old knitting magazines also contain lots of useful information. Look for interesting basic structures that you can turn into letters or embed your font into.

Knit several swatches with different sizes of needle (based on the needle size given on the ball band) to find out which needles are ideal for you. Then wash them, in order to determine how much they will shrink. So you can use them as guides, photograph and measure the swatches before and after washing.

Test the effects of various foreground and background colors with the swatch, too. The relief structure of the slipped stitches creates added shadow effects, which are very difficult to anticipate in the layout.

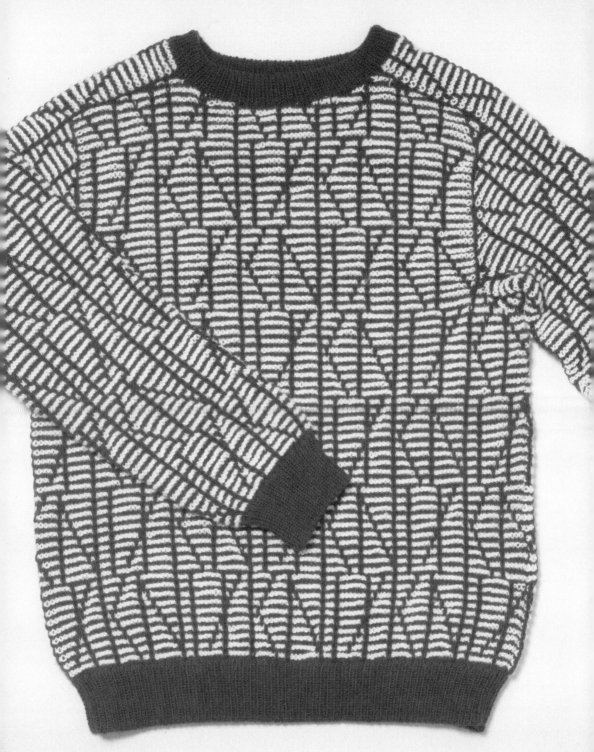

FONT: CUSTOM
TECHNIQUE: SLIP STITCHES AS A LINE [→ P.112]
MATERIALS: LANG YARNS MERINO 120 (3.5-MM/US 4/UK 9 NEEDLES)

SLIP-STITCH SWEATER

Sizes: 46/48–50/52–54 (S/M/L)
Actual measurements: chest 42/44/46 in.
(106/112/116 cm), length 26/27/28 in.
(66/68/70 cm). (Instructions are given by size
and separated with a slash. If only one number
is given, this applies to all three sizes.)

MATERIALS

Yarn: Lang Yarns Merino 120 (100% pure new
wool), 500/550/600 g in red 34.0060 (color 1),
500/550/600 g in off-white 34.0002 (color 2)
Needles: 3.5 mm (US 4/UK 9)

PATTERN I (RIB)

Knit in red with 3.5-mm (US 4/UK 9) nds.
Row 1: K1, P1 (repeat). Row 2 and all other rows:
knit stitches as they appear (knit the knit
stitches, purl the purl stitches).

PATTERN II (PATTERN REPEAT)

Work odd double rows in stockinette stitch and
even double rows in garter stitch (with the motif
from the slip-stitch pattern). The letters are
formed in the even double slip-stitch rows as
shown in the pattern.

PATTERN REPEAT GAUGE

Over 4×4 in. (10×10 cm) with:
3.5-mm (US 4/UK 9) nds: 25 sts/42 rows (= 21 DR)
4-mm (US 6/UK 8) nds: 23 sts/41 rows (= 20.5 DR)

BACK

Rib: cast on 121/127/133 sts in red and knit 2.25
in. (6 cm) in patt I. *Pattern repeat:* cont in patt II,
deciding in advance which part of repeat is to be
in the middle. *Shape armholes:* bind off 3/4/5 sts
at beg of next 2 rows when back measures 16 in.
(40 cm) from cast-on edge, then bind off 1×3,
2×2, 3×1 sts for all three sizes. Cont to work rem
95/99/103 sts. When armhole measures 8/8.5/9
in. (20/22/24 cm), bind off 4, 5, 4, 5, 4, 5 sts for
shoulders at each end of next 6 rows.

Shape neck: at the same time bind off center
11/15/19 sts on RS for neck when working
fourth bind-off. On next 2 rows bind off 7/8 sts
on both sides of center sts.

FRONT

Knit as for back with exception of neck. *Shape
neck:* shape shoulders and neck simultaneously.
Bind off center 11/15/19 sts and at the same
time 5, 4, 3, 2, 1 sts at each end of next 5 rows.

SLEEVES

Rib: cast on 61/65/69 sts in red and knit 2.25 in.
(6 cm) in patt I. *Pattern repeat:* inc 8 sts evenly in
row 1 and distribute patt from middle. Inc 15 × 1
st every 1 in. (2.5 cm). For the word *KNIT*, repeat
patt and knit armhole gussets so that vertical
lines of letters *K* and *N* form lines of shoulder
yoke (sts 19–38 in. center). Knit patt sts plus edge
sts for sewing up.

FINISHING

Block pieces, place under a damp cloth, and
leave to dry. Close seams, inserting last 5 in.
(13 cm) of sleeves as armhole gusset. Pick up
130/138/148 sts in red along neck edge and knit
2.25–2.5 in. (6–7 cm) in. patt I. Bind off. Fold in
half of rib and sew to sweater body. Then sew
in sleeves and close side and sleeve seams in
mattress stitch.

ABBREVIATIONS

beg = beginning	P = purl
cont = continue	patt = pattern
DR = double row	rem = remaining
inc = increase	RS = right side
K = knit	sl st = slip stitch(es)
nds = needles	st(s) = stitch(es)

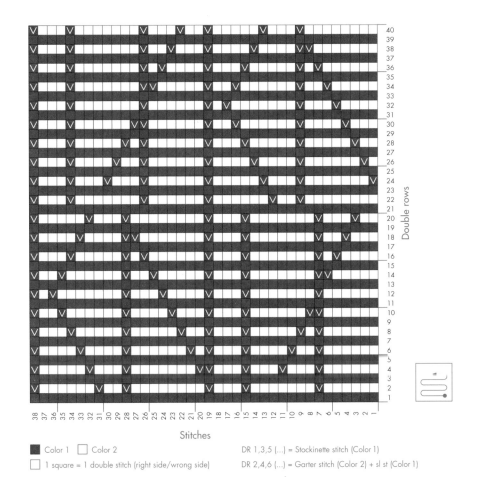

Double rows

Stitches

Color 1 ☐ Color 2

☐ 1 square = 1 double stitch (right side/wrong side)

DR 1,3,5 (…) = Stockinette stitch (Color 1)

DR 2,4,6 (…) = Garter stitch (Color 2) + sl st (Color 1)

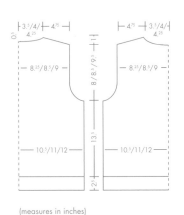

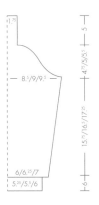

(measures in inches)

CHILDREN'S SWEATERS

It's no coincidence that there are multitudes of knitting patterns for babies and children on the market. Small hats and sweaters are also relatively easy to knit with little experience, which means you need less time and fewer materials. They make good beginner's projects where you can hone your *typeknitting* skills on a small scale—and are great gifts!

Adapting a current knitting pattern has the advantage that you can source the materials it uses. Yarn collections often change their range of colors. Check in advance how many balls of which color are available or look for a similar yarn. It's best to sketch your motif onto a paper pattern that you can directly compare with your work as you knit.

CHILD'S INTARSIA SWEATER

Sizes: 2–3 /4–5 /6 years
= 92–98/104–110/116
Actual measurements: chest 27/29/31 in.
(68/74/80 cm), length 15/16/18 in. (37/41/45 cm)

MATERIALS

Yarn: Lang Yarns Yak (50/50% yak/merino)
Main body: 150/150/200 g = 3/3/4 balls of melon 772.0029; *arms/rib:* 50 g = 1 ball each of beige 772.0026, light olive 772.0197, and Atlantic 772.0074; *letter:* 50 g = 1 ball of off-white 772.0094; *needles:* 4.5- (US/UK 7) and 5-mm (US 8/UK 6); 1 short 4.5-mm (US/UK 7) circular needle

PATTERN

Pattern I: 4.5-mm (US/UK 7) nds: K1, P1
Pattern II: 5-mm (US 8/UK 6) nds: st st

SWATCH

Over 4×4 in. (10×10 cm) with:
5-mm (US 8/UK 6) nds: 19 sts/24 rows

BACK

Cast on 65/69/73 sts in. Atlantic using 4.5-mm (US/UK 7) nds. Knit patt I until rib measures 2.25 in. (6 cm). Cont in patt II and melon. Place marker on both sides 9.5/10.5/12 in. (24/27/30 cm) from cast-on edge (measured hanging). Cont in patt.

Shoulders: 5/5.5/6 in. (13/14/15 cm) from markers bind off 2×10 sts/1×10 sts + 1×11 sts/2×11 sts at each end of every 2nd row. Bind off rem 25/27/29 sts for neck.

FRONT

Knit as for back. *Motif:* as intarsia in off-white. *Shape neck:* bind off center 9/11/13 sts 12/14/15 in. (31/35/38 cm) from cast-on edge and 1×3 sts, 2×2 sts, and 1×1 sts on both sides of center opening on every 2nd row. Shape shoulders as for back at the same height.

SLEEVES

Right sleeve: cast on 38/40/42 sts in melon using 4.5-mm (US/UK 7) nds. Knit patt I until rib measures 2.25 in. (6 cm). Cont in patt II and light olive. To shape sleeves inc 7/8/9 × 1 st on every alt 6th and 8th row on both sides = 52/56/60 sts. Loosely bind off all sts 11/12/13.5 in. (28/31/34 cm) from cast-on edge. *Left sleeve:* Knit as for right sleeve in melon and beige.

FINISHING

Close seams, leaving side seams open at rib. *Neck rib:* with circular needle and Atlantic pick up approx. 70/74/80 sts (back = 28/30/33 sts, front = 42/44/47 sts). Knit patt I in the round until rib measures 1.5 in. (4 cm). Loosely bind off all sts. Set in sleeves between markers on front and back.

FONT: ELEMENTAR SANS B [→ P.193]
TECHNIQUE: INTARSIA [→ P.92], STOCKINETTE STITCH [→ P.78]
MATERIALS: LANG YARNS YAK (4.5-MM/US/UK 7 AND 5-MM/US 8/UK 6 NEEDLES)

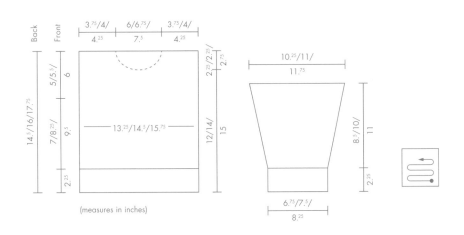

(measures in inches)

ABBREVIATIONS

cont = continue	patt = pattern
inc = increase	rem = remaining
nds = needles	st(s) = stitch(es)

CHILD'S SLIP-STITCH SWEATER

The pattern for this sweater is based on child's sweater 1 (materials: Lang Yarns Merino 120, 3.5-mm / US 4/UK 9 needles). However, slip stitches are used to make the pattern structure here [→ p.116]. *Calcula* [→ p.198] is the script used, placed behind a grid that vertically divides the letter stem into five pixels or stitches. Stitches 1, 3, 5 are knitted in white; stitches 2 and 4 are slip stitches. Knit the front,

back and sleeves first [1]. Then join the shoulder seams. Pick up and knit stitches from the neck edge for the neck ribbing and continue in rib. When the rib measures 1.5 in. (4 cm), loosely bind off all stitches. Then make the sleeves [2]. To finish, sew up the side and sleeve seams in mattress stitch.

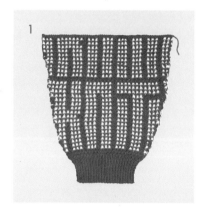

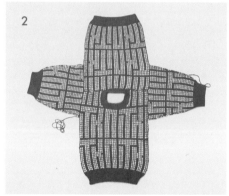

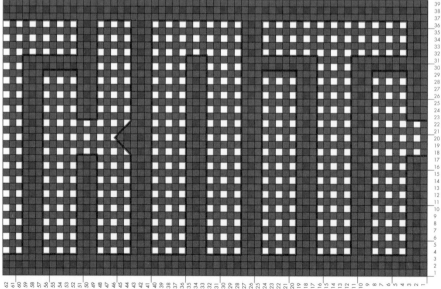

Double rows

Stitches

■ Color 1   ■ Color 2   □ Color 3   DR 1,3,5 (...) = Garter stitch (Color 1)
□ 1 square = 1 double stitch (right side/wrong side)   DR 2,4,6 (...) = Garter stitch (Color 2+3) + sl st (Color 1)

CHILD'S FAIR ISLE SWEATER

This classic Fair Isle sweater is an advanced project for experienced knitters. The sweater is knit in stockinette stitch in the round using the Fair Isle technique and is seamless except for an approximately 1.5-in. (4-cm) seam under the arms. (Materials: Lang Yarns Merino 120, 3.5-mm/US 4/UK 9 needles).

The front and back are knitted as one piece with circular needles, as are the two sleeves. So that these become wider the further up the sleeve you work, increase two stitches per round along the inner edge at regular intervals. Start the pattern on all three sections about 1.25 in. (3 cm) before the armhole.

At the start of the armhole bind off around six stitches on both sides of the front and back and the sleeves (these will be sewn together to finish). Then place all parts of the sweater on one circular needle in the following order: *front, sleeve, back, sleeve.*

Continue in the pattern in the round and knit four raglan decreases where the front/back and sleeves meet (decrease eight stitches in each round). Knit 17 decreases every second round and 9 decreases in each round. Adapt the type pattern to fit. You are left with the stitches for the neck. Knit the neck rib from the remaining stitches at the front and back, fold in half of the rib, and hem it to the sweater top.

Yarn markers are very useful to indicate the end of each pattern repeat (every 14 stitches) [1]. Make sure not to pull the stranded yarn too tight at the back and don't leave it too loose. When knitting more than seven stitches in one color, weave the other color into the back approximately every three stitches so that the strands aren't too long. To do so, simply twist one yarn around the other.

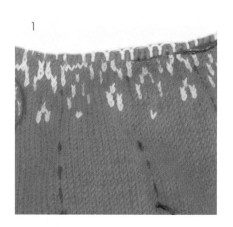

1

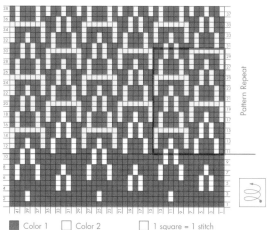

Color 1   Color 2   1 square = 1 stitch

Pattern Repeat

VII.

GRAPHIC
RESOURCES

Fonts and chart templates

After several attempts at knitting, you will learn to identify with increasing ease which typefaces readily lend
themselves to knitting, which are better knitted up large,
and which also work in smaller formats. The following
pages contain a handful of pixel font classics and several
reinterpretations. Many type designers and type found-
ries have preview functions on their websites where you
can gain a good impression of the fonts or even create
your own small test graphic.

ABCDEFG
HIJKLMN
OPQRSTU
VWXYZ#/

PRINT CHAR 21 (APPLE][)   DESIGN: SIGNETICS   KREATIVE KORPORATION

PET ME 2Y (COMMODORE 64)   DESIGN: LEONARD TRAMIEL   KREATIVE KORPORATION

PET ME 2X (COMMODORE 64)   DESIGN: LEONARD TRAMIEL   KREATIVE KORPORATION

GEM DESKTOP 2.0   DESIGN: DIGITAL RESEARCH

ELEMENTAR SANS B (09 31 2)   DESIGN: GUSTAVO FERREIRA   TYPOTHEQUE

ELEMENTAR SANS A (10 11 1)   DESIGN: GUSTAVO FERREIRA   TYPOTHEQUE

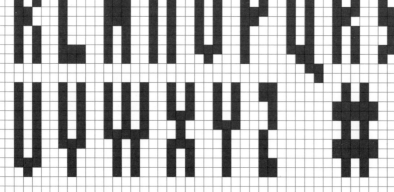

ELEMENTAR SANS B (14 12 1)   DESIGN: GUSTAVO FERREIRA   TYPOTHEQUE

ELEMENTAR SANS B (17 11 4)   DESIGN: GUSTAVO FERREIRA   TYPOTHEQUE

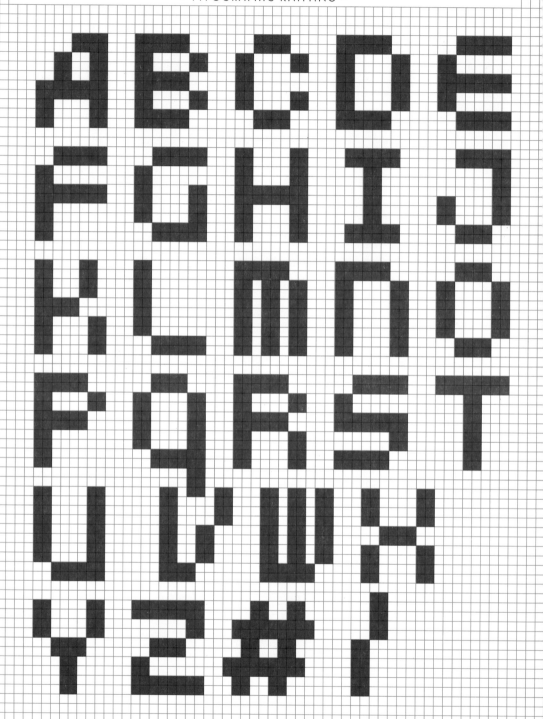

TWOSTROKE A 4-4   DESIGN: PAUL McNEIL, HAMISH MUIR   MUIRMcNEIL

INTERSECT A 4-4   DESIGN: PAUL McNEIL, HAMISH MUIR   MUIRMcNEIL

CALCULA SOLID   DESIGN: SHIVA NALLAPERUMAL   TYPOTHEQUE

ALTEREGO BOLD   DESIGN: PIETER VAN ROSMALEN   BOLD MONDAY

OBLONG   DESIGN: RUDY VANDERLANS, ZUZANA LICKO   EMIGRE

LO-RES 12 NARROW   DESIGN: ZUZANA LICKO   EMIGRE

ABCDE
FGHIJKL
MNOPQ
RSTUVW
XYZ#

abcdef
ghijklmn
opqrstu
vwxyz#

FUTUR X   DESIGN: STUDIO LAUCKE SIEBEIN

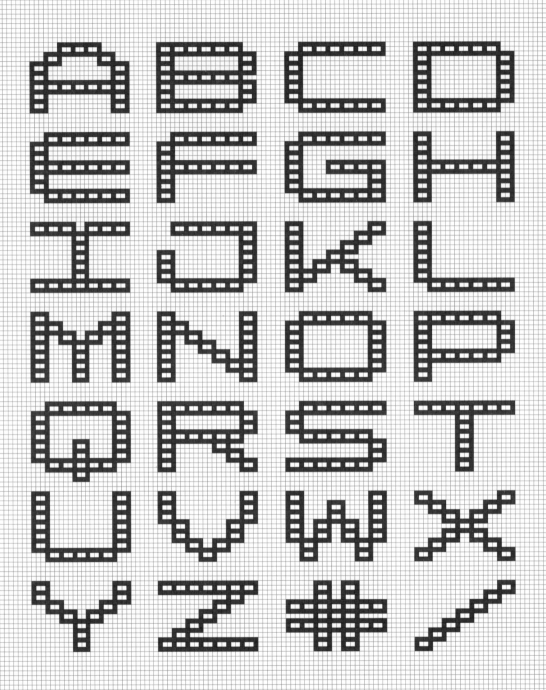

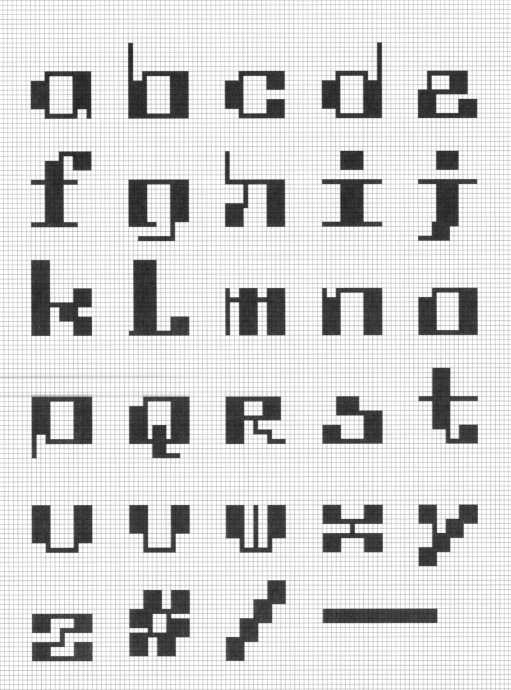

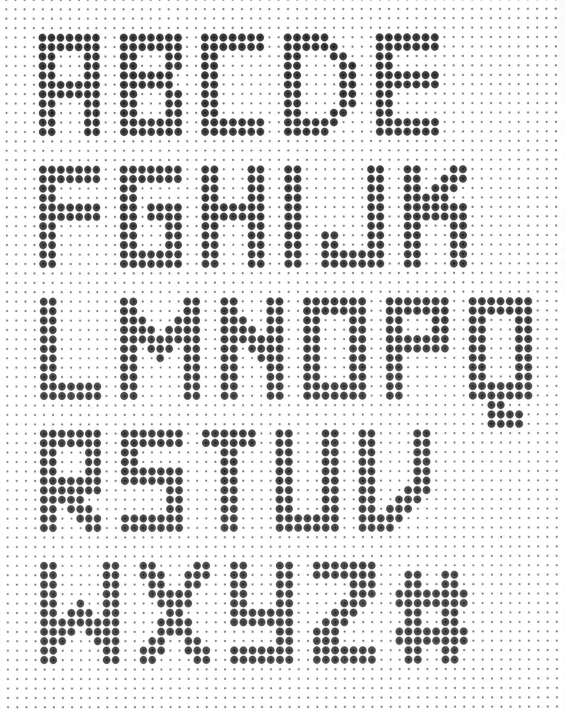

ONLINE ONE PRO DOUBLE   DESIGN: PANOS VASSILIOU   PARACHUTE TYPEFOUNDRY

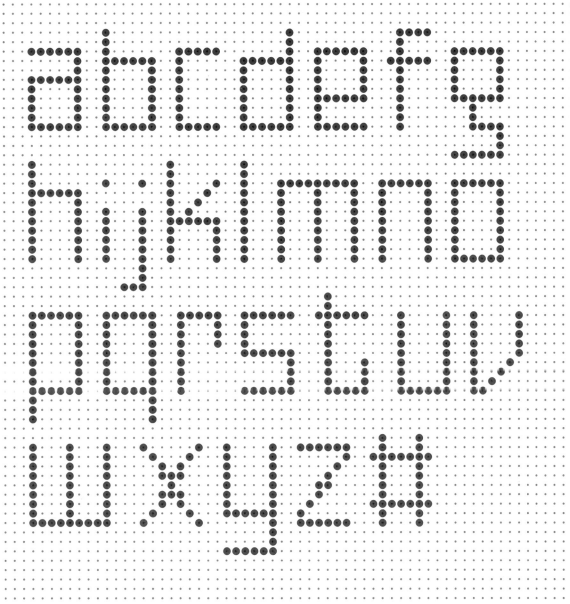

ONLINE ONE PRO SINGLE   DESIGN: PANOS VASSILIOU   PARACHUTE TYPEFOUNDRY

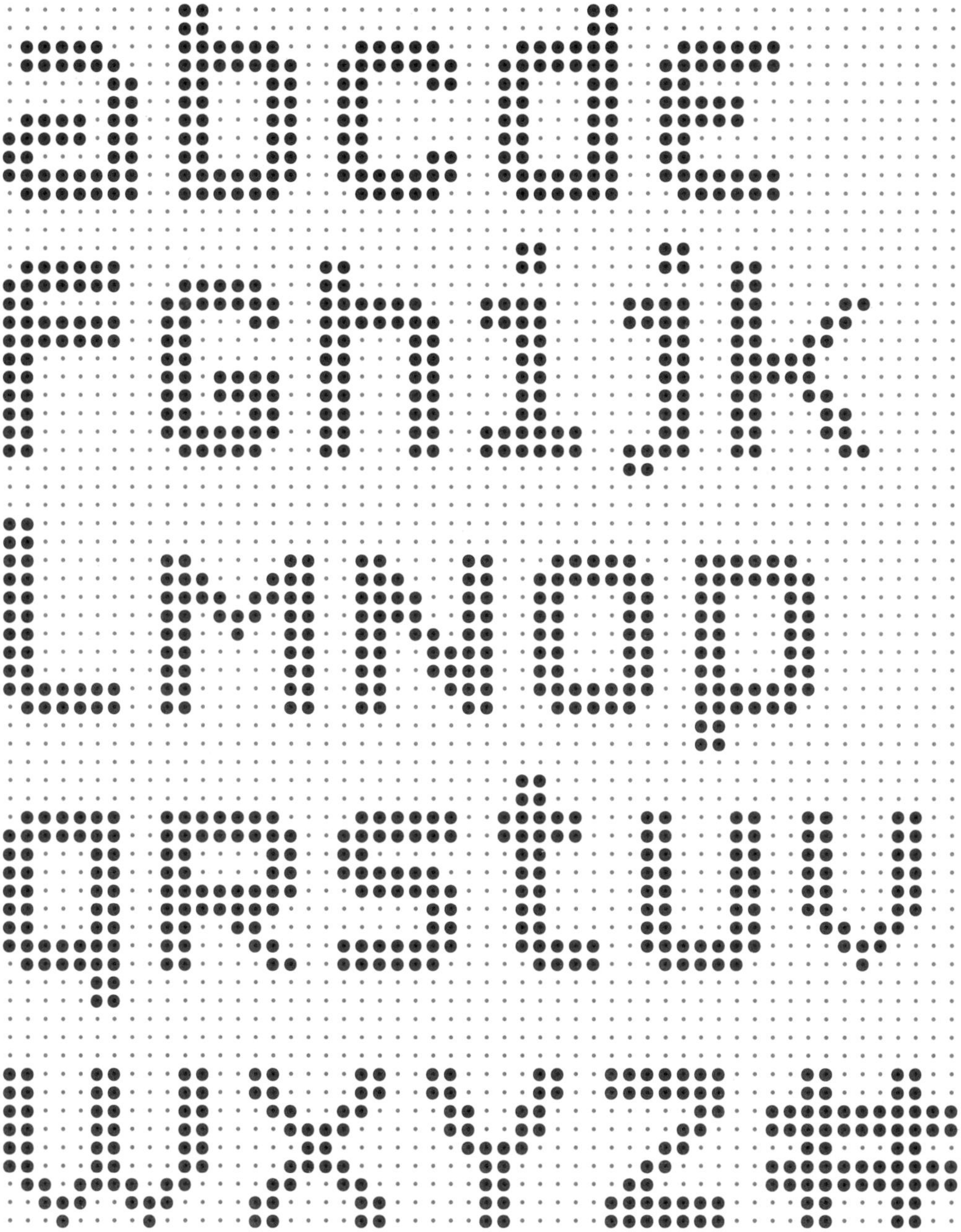

A. POUDRE DESIGN: PHILIPPE APELOIG NOUVELLE NOIRE

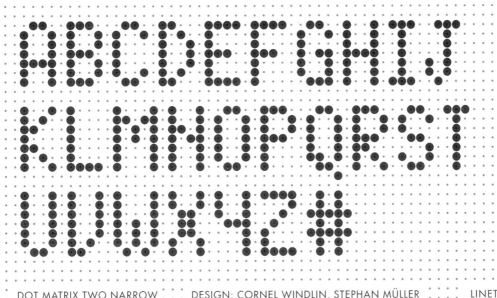

DOT MATRIX TWO NARROW　DESIGN: CORNEL WINDLIN, STEPHAN MÜLLER　LINETO

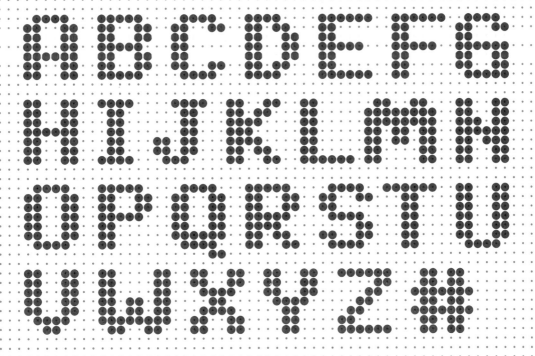

DOT MATRIX TWO EXTENDED　DESIGN: CORNEL WINDLIN, STEPHAN MÜLLER　LINETO

PANOPTICON A   DESIGN: PAUL McNEIL, HAMISH MUIR   MUIRMcNEIL

CHART TEMPLATES

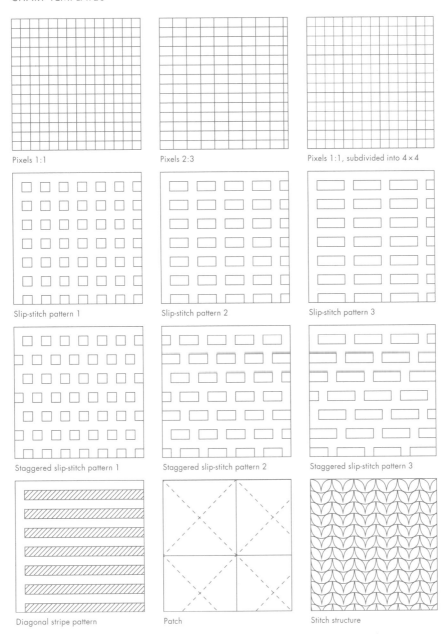

Pixels 1:1

Pixels 2:3

Pixels 1:1, subdivided into 4 × 4

Slip-stitch pattern 1

Slip-stitch pattern 2

Slip-stitch pattern 3

Staggered slip-stitch pattern 1

Staggered slip-stitch pattern 2

Staggered slip-stitch pattern 3

Diagonal stripe pattern

Patch

Stitch structure

You can find all the pattern
templates on www.typeknitting.net

RESOURCES

TYPE FOUNDRIES & STUDIOS

Bold Monday
www.boldmonday.com

Christian Schmalohr Design
www.schmalohrdesign.de

Emigre Fonts
www.emigre.com

Flore Levrouw
www.florelevrouw.com

Kreative Korporation
www.kreativekorp.com/software/fonts

Lineto
www.lineto.com

MuirMcNeil
www.muirmcneil.com

Nouvelle Noire
www.nouvellenoire.ch

Parachute Type Foundry
www.parachutefonts.com

RP Digital Type Foundry
www.radimpesko.com

Studio Laucke Siebein
www.studio-laucke-siebein.com

Typecuts
www.typecuts.com

Typotheque
www.typotheque.com

Walking Chair Design Studio
www.walking-chair.com

FONT MARKETPLACES

Fontstand—try fonts for free or rent them
www.fontstand.com

MyFonts
www.myfonts.com

FONT & GRAPHIC TOOLS

Bitfontmaker 2
www.pentacom.jp

Fontlab
www.fontlab.com

FontStruct
www.fontstruct.com

Glyphs
www.glyphsapp.com

Pixlr
www.pixlr.com

Vectoraster
www.lostminds.com/vectoraster7

CHART AND PATTERN TOOLS

Free online graph paper
www.incompetech.com/graphpaper

KnitPro 2.0—pattern translator
www.microrevolt.org/knitPro

Knitting graph paper
www.sweaterscapes.com/land-chart-paper.htm

www.theknittingsite.com/knitting-graph-paper

KNITTING NETWORK

Ravelry—a knit and crochet community
www.ravelry.com

KNITTING BLOGS

Fruity Knitting
www.fruityknitting.com

Knit and Nibble
www.knitnibble.com/blog

Knitting Letters: A to Z
www.unionpurl.blogspot.com

Typeknits
www.instagram.com/typeknits

KNITTING PATTERNS

Butzerla—double-face knitting
Meret Dützberger
www.butzeria.ch

Hello Yarn—knitting patterns
Adrian Bizilia
www.helloyarn.com

Alasdair Post-Quinn—double knitting
www.double-knitting.com

Jessica Tromp—Norwegian knitting
www.jessica-tromp.nl/norwegian
knittingknitwearnorse.htm

Woolly Thoughts—illusion knitting
Pat Ashforth and Steve Plummer
www.woollythoughts.com

www.ravelry.com/patterns/library/
illusion-love-cushion

KNITTING TUTORIALS

Basic and advanced knitting techniques
www.weareknitters.com/learn-knit

Knitaholics—video tutorials with eliZZZa
www.knitaholics.net/all-english/

Learn to Knit a Mitered Square—knitpicks
www.youtube.com/watch?v=QVmJfSNfp6k

Mitered Squares—VeryPink Knits
www.verypink.com/2012/03/07/
mitered-squares/

Illusion/shadow knitting
www.garnstudio.com/video.php?id=990

www.illusionknitting.woollythoughts.com/
videotutorials.html

Illusion knitting tutorial for creating
complex image patterns
www.illusionknitting.woollythoughts.com/
tigertutorial.html.

BOOKS

Sabrina Gschwandtner, *KnitKnit: Profiles + Projects from Knitting's New Wave,* Stewart, Tabori & Chang (2007)

Horst Schulz, *Patchwork Knitting,* Saprotex International (2000)

Horst Schulz, *New Patchwork Knitting: Fashion for Children,* Saprotex International (2000)

ACKNOWLEDGMENTS

Lots of people have contributed to the development and realization of this book. I would like to heartily thank the following:

My family, especially my wife, Irene, for her patience and support in all fields.

Princeton Architectural Press for making this English edition possible: Parker Menzimer and Paul Wagner.

Verlag Hermann Schmidt:
Karin and Bertram Schmidt-Friderichs, Lisa Bartelmeß, Lina Himpel, Sandra Mulitze, Brigitte Raab, Clara Scheffler, Jutta Schober, Birgit Severin.

Linda Suter for the beautiful photos.

All of the professional knitters:
Christel Artz, Pat Ashforth, Evi Balzar, Veronika Beckh, Adrian Bizilia, Meret Bützberger, Francisca Carrion Navas, Valentina Devine, Maja Enderlin, Monika Faul, Kerstin Hering, Martina Hoschatt, Sari Järvinen, Renate Korpus, Jane Lataille, Astrid Mania, Margrith Maurer-Fedier, Rosetta Meyer, Cornelia Mindner, Hisae Mizutani, Steve Plummer, Michaela Renz, Frauke Riecke, Eveline Riefer-Rucht, Saiko Ryusui, Irene Schlömer, Horst Schulz, Therese Strand, Sunshine Wong, Conceptual Knitting Circle, Knitting in Los Alamos.

All of the type designers:
Philippe Apeloig, Rebecca Bettencourt, Peter Bilak, Gustavo Ferreira, Dirk Laucke, Flore Levrouw, Zuzana Licko, Paul McNeil, Max Miedinger, Hamish Muir, Stephan Müller, Shiva Nallaperumal, Karl Nawrot, Radim Pesko, Fidel Peugeot, Pieter van Rosmalen, Christian Schmalohr, Johanna Siebein, Anton Studer, Andrea Tinnes, Leonard Tramiel, Clovis Vallois, Rudy Vanderlans, Panos Vassiliou, Cornel Windlin and the type and typography class at Burg Giebichenstein University of Art and Design Halle.

Eva Afuhs, Clara Åhlvik, Michael Ammann, Ramón Bill, Joshua Brägger, Otto von Busch, Heike Ebner, Sabine Fabo, Mònica Gaspar, Eva Grimmer, Maike Hamacher, Kerstin Hering, Florian Jakober, Christoffer Joergensen, Garth Johnson, Kasimir, Miriam Koban, Petr Kozusnik, Katja Läuppi, Jan Lindenberg, Yoshito Maeoka, Stefan Mau, Milan, Nestor, Naoko Ogawa, Martin Rohr, Deborah Rozenblum, Rosemarie Schaltegger, Cornelia Schmidt-Bleek, Ben Schmücking, Liane Schommertz, Gaby & Wilhelm Schürmann, Ines Schulz, Chandima Soysa, Michael Stevenson, Jaroslav Toussaint, Tanja Trampe, Saskia von Virág, Imke Volkers, Anna Wehrli.

All of the exhibition/workshop venues:
Museum Bellerive in Zurich, Burg Giebichenstein Kunsthochschule Halle, Garanti Galeri in Istanbul, Institute for Art in Context at the University of the Arts in Berlin, Jönköping County Museum, Röhsska Design Museum in Göteborg, Schürmann Berlin, Social Kitchen in Kyoto, Temporäre Kunsthalle in Berlin, and Wäscherei at Kunstverein Zurich.

My sponsors:
Addi Needles and Lang Yarns.

Photo: Dominik Fricker

ABOUT THE AUTHOR

In *Typographic Knitting*, Rüdiger Schlömer combines his interests and experience as a designer, curator, and exhibition facilitator.

He grew up in Paris, France, and Bremen, Germany, studied Visual Communication in Aachen, Germany, and Art in Context in Berlin, Germany, and has worked in book design, exhibition graphics, experience design, and signage for many years in Zurich, Switzerland.

Focusing on visual conception and design process, he has worked for various museums, companies, and design bureaus, including The Jewish Museum in Berlin, The Military History Museum in Dresden, The Swiss Museum of Transport in Lucerne, and The Werkbund Archive— Museum of Things in Berlin.

In his own initiated projects, he explores communicative formats and para-digital principles, such as hacking or reverse engineering in textiles, notation, and interfacing. He has held workshops at art schools and museums in Japan, Mexico, Norway, Sweden, Switzerland, and Turkey.

His work has appeared in publications such as *Kunstforum International*, *I.D.*, *Form*, and *Spex*, and won several prizes, including the Interactive ZKM Media Art Award (together with Michael Janoschek), the Iconic Award, and the Red Dot Award. His book *Pixel, Patch und Pattern: Typeknitting* received a Certificate of Typographic Excellence from the Type Directors Club NY.

Rüdiger Schlömer lives and works in Zurich, Switzerland.

www.rudigerschlomer.com

Dedication
– For I, K, N, and L

Published by
Princeton Architectural Press
202 Warren Street
Hudson, New York 12534
www.papress.com

Published in Germany with the title
Pixel, Patch und Pattern: Typeknitting
by Verlag Hermann Schmidt.
Verlag Hermann Schmidt © 2018

English edition:
© 2020 Princeton Architectural Press
All rights reserved
Printed and bound in China
23 22 21 20 4 3 2 1 First Edition

No part of this book may be used or reproduced
in any manner without written permission from
the publisher, except in the context of reviews.

Every reasonable attempt has been made
to identify owners of copyright. Errors or
omissions will be corrected in subsequent
editions.

For Princeton Architectural Press:

Project editor: Parker Menzimer
Cover design: Paul Wagner
Translation: Ruth Chitty

Special thanks to: Paula Baver, Janet Behning,
Abby Bussel, Jan Cigliano Hartman, Susan
Hershberg, Kristen Hewitt, Stephanie Holstein,
Lia Hunt, Valerie Kamen, Cooper Lippert,
Jennifer Lippert, Sara McKay, Wes Seeley,
Rob Shaeffer, Sara Stemen, Jessica Tackett,
Marisa Tesoro, and Joseph Weston of Princeton
Architectural Press—Kevin C. Lippert, publisher

Special thanks to Emily Rose O'Keefe for her
insightful assessment of the core audience for
this project.

Concept & graphic design: Rüdiger Schlömer
Photography: Linda Suter / www.lindasuter.ch
Process photos: Maja Enderlin (p. 185),
Flore Levrouw (p. 53), Michaela Renz (p. 184),
Jaroslav Toussaint (pp. 28–29)
Typefaces: Nexus Serif, Futura LT
Cover Image: Selbu Mittens, based on Generic
Norwegian Mittens by Adrian Bizilia, knitted
by Margrith Maurer-Fedier.

Sponsor sources:
Lang Yarns USA: Berroco Inc. / www.berroco.com
Lang Yarns UK / www.langyarns.com
Addi needles / www.addi.de

Project updates and workshop information:
www.typeknitting.net
www.facebook.com/typeknitting
www.instagram.com/typeknitting
www.ravelry.com/groups/typeknitting

Knit and share: #typeknitting

Library of Congress
Cataloging-in-Publication Data:

Names: Schlömer, Rüdiger, author.
Title: Typographic knitting : from pixel to
pattern / [Rüdiger Schlömer].
Other titles: Pixel, Patch und Pattern. English
Description: New York : Princeton Architectural
Press, 2019. | Translation
of: Pixel, Patch und Pattern. | Includes
bibliographical references.
Identifiers: LCCN 2019008462 | ISBN
9781616898540 (pbk. : alk. paper)
Subjects: LCSH: Knitting—Patterns. | Lettering.
| Graphic design (Typography)
Classification: LCC TT820 .S292 2019 | DDC
746.43/2041—dc23
LC record available at https://lccn.loc.
gov/2019008462